The Youngest Tigers in the Sky

The Youngest Tigers in the Sky

by

William W. Wyper

FIRST EDITION

Library of Congress Catalog Number 80-51438

ISBN 0-9604386-0-2

Printed in the United States of America

Distributed by
AERO PUBLISHERS, INC.
329 West Aviation Road, Fallbrook, CA 92028

Foreword

Bandit sighted at nine-o'clock level. The fighter pilot instinctively reacts. Left hand advancing the throttle, right hand moving the stick left and back while his left foot shoves hard on the rudder pedal. G-forces push him down in his seat as he turns to meet his enemy head-on.

As they flash past, each man has an option. He can keep his throttle bent to the firewall and try to escape or he can rack it around and try again. If one goes straight, the other pilot most assuredly will crank his bird around and take up the chase.

A turning option is also available. If they both turn toward the same direction, another head-on pass is inevitable. If they turn toward opposite directions, the chase begins in earnest.

Tight turns sap off an aircraft's speed and the man being chased certainly doesn't want to be a slow-moving target so he trades altitude for speed. The turning twisting ballet constantly descends. No matter what altitude the encounter begins, if it lasts long enough it will end up right on the deck. Those are the rules of the game, . . . of aerial combat. Whether it's a Spad over Chateau-Thierry, a P-51 chasing a Tony over Osaka, an F-86 battling a MIG over the Yalu, or an F-4 over Vietnam, the precise sequence of the dog fight remains the same. The sequence is dictated not by man, but by the physical laws of motion, energy and gravity. But the outcome is dictated by man and his machine, by his ability to outfly and outshoot his adversary.

Another axiom regarding war in the air: the sky has always been the exclusive battle arena of the young. Unfortunately, all of the young men who struggled for the chance to do battle in the sky weren't afforded the opportunity to become great aces, but they were no less tigers. Some were killed during their struggle to become tigers. Others were killed, not by the enemy, but by their own inability to master the unforgiving demands of their specialized profession. This book is a reminiscence of experiences of one of those once-young tigers in the sky. It is dedicated to all of the young men who fought in the skies, especially those who never lived to reminisce.

Author's Note

As I reached for the door to enter the base headquarters the door swung open and two very young slick sleeve privates came rushing out. Upon seeing me, they jerked to attention and gave me their very best newly learned salutes. I returned their salutes and they scrambled away. I guess they hadn't run head-on into a commissioned officer before, but the expressions on their faces made me feel much older than my twenty-one years. They were probably eighteen and I was twenty-one but there was more than three years between us. We were separated by a war that had just ended. Being their age just three years earlier had allowed me the privilege of participating in a portion of that war, with some of the youngest tigers in the sky.

W. W. W.

The Youngest Tigers in the Sky

Contents

Illustrations by the author.

In the late thirties and early forties, one of the prerequisites for young men entering the U.S. military pilot training was the completion of at least two years of college. This requirement prevailed for both the Army Air Corps and the Navy until there weren't enough two-year college men available to fill the war time quotas of the expanded and accelerated flight training programs. As mobilization was getting into high gear, the Army Air Force's two-year college requirement for aviation cadets was waived for young men between eighteen and twenty-seven who could pass a special written examination.

Many of the young men, eager to join up and fight for their country, eyed the flying branches because of their much publicized glamour. My interest in aviation far exceeded any desire motivated by the war time propaganda. As long as I could remember, the thought of flying an airplane, and particularly a pursuit plane, represented the epitome of achievement — an accomplishment which prior to the war would have been impossible to attain. But, fate provided the opportunity. I had just graduated from high school and was approaching my eighteenth birthday.

Some older high school acquaintances had already applied for entrance into the Army Air Forces Aviation Cadet Training program. Their stories of how tough the written examination was plus the extremely difficult-to-pass physical examination all but destroyed my hopes of ever becoming a military pilot.

That long-awaited first step finally arrived. With about forty other young men, I went to the Army Air Corps Los Angeles office to take the written examination.

A young lieutenant, without wings, told us what we were to do. The test forms were then passed out to each of us. The timekeeper was a sergeant who told us when to start. It was sort of a generalized I.Q. test covering all sorts of things. One section was on history, one was on current events, one was on mathematics. Another was on mechanics, logic and so on. Time was finally called and the papers were collected. Having known some pretty bright fellows who had failed this very test, I couldn't keep from being very worried. Although I expected the worst, I was absolutely positive that nobody in that room wanted to become a pursuit pilot more than I did. We all just sat there and waited while our papers were being graded. After what seemed an interminable length of time, the lieutenant came back into the room and said, "Mr. Wyper." My hopes plummeted, but I managed a meek "Yes Sir." He said, "Mr. Wyper, you got today's highest score." About half of the group failed to make the passing minimum.

A couple of days later I reported back to the same building to take the much dreaded physical examination. The "six three" physical presented no challenge until it came time for my left eye to read letters twenty millimeters high, twenty feet away. Try as I might, my effort was reduced to guessing and apparently my guesses weren't good enough. The examining doctor, a civilian, asked me how much rest I had the previous night. If he was looking for an excuse as to why I was failing his eye examination, I certainly wasn't going to let him down. Anticipating taking this very important physical, I naturally had plenty of rest the previous night, but interpreting his question as a quest for an excuse, I responded accordingly. He said that my eyes were probably tired and that I should get some rest and try again in a few days. My next try at that eye chart was not much better. The kindly doctor said that I probably hadn't given my eyes enough rest so he advised me to go home, get more rest and then come back and try again. Looking back on it now, I think he might have been giving me a chance to memorize the chart but I was too naive to catch on. I came back the third time and tried again, but to no avail. By this time the doctor was aware of my eagerness to get into cadet training so he said that he would put down 20/20 but that I must realize the risk I would be taking, of failing to pass a subsequent eye test and consequently be eliminated. I couldn't thank him enough and said that I would be more than happy to take the chance. The funny thing was that I never had a problem with any of the subsequent eye examinations. The military doctors must have figured that we had eyes like eagles, otherwise we wouldn't have gotten in.

First step for the future tigers of the Army Air Corps was the Aviation Cadet Classification Center. They poured in by the trainload to each of the three classification centers. During World War II, the Army Air Force had three training commands, the Southwest at Santa Ana, California, the Southeast at Nashville, Tennessee, and the Central Training Command located near San Antonio, Texas. I was happy over my assignment to the Central Training Command because I considered San Antonio the true home of the Army Air Corps.

After all, the legendary fields, Randolph, Kelly and Brooks, were all right here at San Antone.

The San Antonio Aviation Cadet Center — SAACC — always referred to as "Sack" was an enormous place, acres and acres of two-story barracks and administrative buildings. But Sack was only part of the huge complex. Directly adjacent to Sack was the preflight facility, more acres and acres of two-story barracks, the place to which we all hoped to soon be assigned.

The purpose of the Classification Center was to weed out any misfits, any man that they didn't think would be a worthwhile investment to become a commissioned officer qualified to participate in aerial warfare. A man could be disqualified for a wide variety of reasons; medical, mental, coordination, attitude and so on. We were to be tested, analyzed, scrutinized, to be eliminated or to be classified for training as a bombardier, navigator or pilot. Young men from all walks of life suddenly found themselves thrust into a struggle for the mere chance to begin training which hopefully would lead to silver wings and gold bars. This was the first introduction to military life for most of us, but there were exceptions. Instead of reporting in civilian clothes, there were a few in uniform, some with stripes on their sleeves, some with ribbons on their chests and some even with wings — wings of aircrew members. As enlisted men they had qualified as aerial gunners. They had applied for aviation cadet training and were now getting their chance along with us recent civilians. Most of us came directly from school, some like myself right out of high school, others had been in college.

Processing started immediately. We were assigned to barracks. Each floor of each barrack was designated as a specific Flight. The ground army had its squads, platoons, companies, battalions, regiments and divisions, but this was the Air Force. We were assigned to elements, flights, squadrons, groups and wings, the same way that all of the flying units were organized. Our personal life and our Flight became one and the same throughout our stay in the classification center. We were marched in our flight formation to virtually every activity of the day. Sometimes we sang when we marched. Our quickly memorized repertoire included, "I've Been Working on the Railroad", "Jolly, Jolly Six Pence" and a very short set of lyrics that we sang to the tune of "Stars and Stripes Forever", that went:

"Now be kind to your web-footed‚friends,

for a duck may be somebody's mother.

He lives in a creek by a swamp,

where the weather is always damp.

Now you may think this is the end.

Well, it is!"

We marched in our flight to breakfast and back. We marched in our flight to every scheduled processing event. We marched in our flight to take our daily physical training and we did our exercising as a flight. Needless to say, by the time we had been classified, we were pretty well acquainted with the other members of our particular flight.

The processing went on for days. We'd no sooner get back to our barracks, from one place, when another noncommissioned officer would show up and order us to fall out into flight formation on the street beside our barracks. We would then be marched off to another place to take yet another test. Most of the tests were taken individually on a very personalized basis, but we marched as a flight to and from each of the testing locations. Briefings, processing and testing continued from dawn to dusk for what seemed to be an endless number of days.

15

The whole purpose was to save the government's time and money by not trying to fit square pegs into round holes. Even before all of the testing was completed, square pegs were being identified and shipped off to other assignments.

The ominous term G.D.O. was one with which we quickly became familiar. It stood for GroundDuty Only. Every couple of days a new G.D.O. list would be posted on the bulletin boards outside the squadron orderly rooms. With pounding hearts and sweaty palms every cadet applicant would read the list. Upon finding their name on the list a few would actually breathe a sigh of relief and turn away contented with the thought of maybe going to O.C.S., Officer Candidate School, to become a non-flying officer in the Army Air Corps. They had convinced themselves that flying in a war with everybody shooting at them wasn't such a good idea after all. But for the most, finding their name on the G.D.O. list was a heartbreaking experience. More than one young man was seen turning away from the bulletin board with tears in his eyes.

Early in the processing, each cadet applicant was required to rank, on a scale of one to ten, his personal preference for training as a bombardier, navigator and pilot. Many tried to hedge their bet by indicating high interest for all three. Final appointments for those who ranked all three nearly equal presented no problems. But, the fellows who put all their points on becoming a pilot were in for a brainwashing if their tests showed low aptitude for pilot training but satisfactory for bombardier or navigator. If they were selected for bombardier or navigator training, they would be called before a board which always included a veteran bombardier or navigator, whichever was required for the particular brainwashing. The veteran bombardier or navigator would try to convince the disappointed young man that theirs was truly the only way to fly. They were given a choice of either accepting the assigned category of training or being transferred away to some other part of the service. Most of them came away from those meetings thoroughly convinced that their being chosen to become a bombardier or navigator would definitely bring the United States one step closer to achieving ultimate victory.

After filling out reams of questionnaires, submitting to in-depth physical examinations, taking a variety of mental examinations, exhibiting our coordination on the tricky psycho-motor tests, and being intimately interviewed by batteries of psychiatrists, those of us who survived were classified as Aviation Cadets. We were now ready to move across the field and start nine grueling weeks of preflight.

If the purpose of preflight was to equip us mentally and physically for what was to come, they must have felt that we needed a lot. We were schooled in a variety of subjects including math, physics, military science, military strategy, military history and protocol. We ran obstacle courses, cross-country races, played competitive sports, gyrated through hours of calisthenics, marched, drilled, stood inspections, stood guard duty and even drew K.P. But they didn't call it K.P. They called it "Mess Management". Their official line was that if we were to become officers we should know the intricacies of how to prepare and serve food to several hundred at a sitting, in true military style. What we did learn was how to get up at three A.M., to mop messhall floors and how to do all the other menial chores that every soldier knows very well as K.P. We also learned why all mess sergeants were fat. They ate extremely well.

We were introduced to "gigs" and "tours". Gigs were like demerits which could easily be acquired by a cadet who breached any of the many rules — some written and some unwritten. Once acquired, gigs could only be eliminated by "walking them off." This was accomplished by a method called tours. A tour was one uninterrupted hour of marching at attention with a rifle, around the quadrangle in front of the the squadron headquarters building. Sunday afternoons, the quadrangle became a particularly popular spot. Instead of one or two cadets, quite often a whole line would be silently marching in single file around and around. A few of the worst offenders were confronted with a real problem. They had piled up more gigs than they had free time in which to march them off. They were the poor souls who found themselves marching

19

around the quandrangle in the middle of the night while the rest of the base slept. That is of course except for their fellow cadets who were mopping the messhall floors and those other cadets who were marching back and forth with loaded rifles around the perimeter of the base doing their stint of guard duty.

The weekly full dress parades at Preflight were really impressive. All of the flights, squadrons, groups and wings, both upper and lower class, participated. It was truly a magnificent sight, twelve thousand young men standing rigidly at attention waiting the command to step out, the visors of their hats two finger widths away from their noses, their white-gloved hands pressed against the side seams of their trousers, the cadet officers with their sabres drawn smartly against their right shoulders. The commissioned officer in charge would give the word to the ranking cadet officer who would then shout at the top of his lungs, "Sound Off." The band would commence. It seemed that all Air Force bands had a repertoire of two pieces, "Off We Go into the Wild Blue Yonder" and "Colonel Bogey". The next command, also shouted at the top of his lungs, was "Pass in Review."

Being a cadet officer was looked upon by most of us as a thankless task. It was a voluntary position requiring extra work. It was a job that ninety-nine percent of the future flyers wanted no part of. I imagine that when they were in grade school, many of them were the special monitors — the teacher's pets. In spite of their extra effort, cadet officers got "washed out" all along the way just like any cadet who failed to pass a required objective. And on graduation day, their gold bars weren't any shinier than the rest of ours.

A required milestone which all cadets had to pass was the high-altitude chamber. This first session inside the low-pressure altitude chamber served two purposes; one, it tested our ability to function at high altitude and to withstand the transitions up and back down, and two, to demonstrate the deadly effects of hypoxia — the lack of oxygen. At the aeromedical building we were fitted with oxygen masks, the same type worn by all aircrews. We wore cloth aviator's helmets onto which the masks were attached. A wire inside the rubber part of the mask that covered the nose could be bent to fit the individual shape of each man's face. After the technicians had fitted the masks, they moved a cotton Q-tip, saturated with camphor, all around the edge of the mask while we breathed through the open end of the hose which dangled a foot and a half below our face. If we smelled the camphor, the technician would make some more adjustments to the nose section.

We couldn't help but have some apprehension as we stepped through the small opening into that ominous chamber that resembled a section of oversize pipe. There were about ten of us including a technician who also went inside. The heavy steel door was closed and locked. We could hear the bolts being tightened. We sat on bench type seats with our backs to the wall, facing each other. After the technician made sure that all of our masks were properly connected to the oxygen hoses, he sat down and hooked up his own. He also had a microphone in his mask which fed a little speaker inside the chamber so we could hear him tell us what was going on. There was a glass porthole in one end of the chamber through which a doctor peered in at us making us feel even more apprehensive. On the wall at one end was an oversize altimeter which we all watched as the air was being pumped out of the chamber. The needle on the altimeter moved quite rapidly to 20,000 feet and stopped. The technician explained that because of the higher altitude that we were going to, we would experience certain bodily sensations, especially the escaping of any gases that might be trapped in our bowels. That's probably the only place in the world where you could be shut inside a very small room with nine other guys — all farting — and not be bothered by any odors, because we were breathing our life-sustaining air from another source. The technician also explained that the thinner air might cause ear and teeth discomfort. Air trapped inside teeth fillings could become very painful at high altitude and eardrums could even rupture during rapid descents if the nasal passages to the inner ears were not open to equalize the difference in pressure.

The needle on the big altimeter started turning again as more air was drawn out of the chamber. This time it stopped at 30,000 feet. He explained that aircrew members must be extremely wary of their own condition when flying at high altitude. In bombers, the crew members could keep an eye on each other for any signs that anyone might not be getting enough oxygen but in fighter planes, where the man would be all by himself, the problem was more critical. The reason being that the individual does not normally realize when he is not getting enough oxygen. The first thing affected is your brain and when that goes goofy how can you be expected to know what is happening and how to correct the trouble. Fighter pilots were constantly reminded of this danger so as a sort of exercise to keep track of their mental condition, on the way up to high altitude, many fighter pilots would mentally add up the numbers on the little compass correction card mounted on their instrument panel. They would memorize the sum total of those numbers. Then, every once in a while, during their time at high altitude, they would mentally add up those numbers again. If they got an answer different from the one previously memorized, they would start checking their oxygen regulator and hose connections. To vividly demonstrate the effects of hypoxia, lack of oxygen, the technician asked for a volunteer. He was handed a pad of paper and a pencil and told to start writing his name. He started at the top of the page and very neatly wrote down his name. The technician then told him to remove his oxygen mask and continue to write his name, over and over. His reactions were comical and of course very frightening. He started to laugh over his inability to write properly. His pencil was scrawling all over the pad and ran clear off of it. Then his head fell to one side and he was out cold. The technician, standing right beside him, immediately slapped the mask back on his face. He came to and looked around the chamber if as much as to say, "What happened?" When shown the pad of paper, he had no recollection of writing anything beyond the first couple of neat lines. We all got the picture.

After four-and-a-half weeks of Preflight, we became the upper class. With this honor came our first "open post," a twelve-hour Sunday pass from noon to midnight. The buses for San Antonio were packed.

The streets of San Antonio were jammed with servicemen from all of the surrounding bases, but this overcrowded situation was somewhat alleviated for the aviation cadets. A private "cadet club" was operated on the mezzanine of the Gunther Hotel in downtown San Antonio. I'm not sure what inspired its inception, but I am sure of one function that was served by the cadet club in the Gunter Hotel. It kept a lot of very drunk aviation cadets off the streets of San Antonio.

One of the subjects we were required to master was radio code. Radio navigational aids are identified by code and sometimes night combat air-to-ground and ground-to-air communications were accomplished through use of flashing lights called "blinker." Learning the dah dits and dit dahs came easy for some, but others had a tougher time. We were taught to hear the dits and dahs as musical phrases rather than trying to count the individual dits and dahs. For example, the code for the letter Q, called QUEEN in the phonetic language at that time, was dah dah dit dah. Its musical phrase was "no balls at all." That system worked very well and most of us got through the audio test with no problem. But passing the blinker test was something else. Hearing the dit dahs was one thing but making out the code from a light silently flashing on and off was really tough. About ninety percent of the class flunked the final blinker test. I was no exception.

The large code room was packed with cadets who had flunked the blinker test. Needless to say this was a tense moment for every man in that room. We had to pass that test or we couldn't graduate from preflight. Final instructions were given. Every eye in that room was riveted on the small light in the far corner of the room. The test was about to begin. You could have heard a pin drop. The light started to flash. But each time the light flashed a very faint buzz could be heard. What a blessing that was. We could actually take the test by audio rather than visual. We all passed. We were very grateful for that faint sound, but I kind of suspect that the establishment didn't want to lose a whole batch of future flyers because of a vague requirement that possibly we would never really use.

As preflight drew to a close it was goodbye to many newly made friends. This was parting of the ways for future bombardiers, navigators and pilots. From here on the training would be specialized.

Primary flying school, especially ours, was like a country club after the gigantic military complex where we had spent the past four months. Grider Field, near Pine Bluff, Arkansas, even looked like a country club. Instead of the standard army two-story barracks, here were rambling single-story buildings that could easily pass for a vacation resort.

We arrived at Grider Field just about time for the evening meal so we were directed to the messhall. Even that was an unexpected surprise. Compared to the huge G.I. messhalls that we had been used to this dining room seemed tiny. But it was adequate to serve the relatively small number of aviation cadets sent here to learn to fly. The messhall was staffed by kindly old ladies that could have been any of our grandmothers. Even the seating was informal, a pleasant contrast to preflight where we even ate by the numbers.

Leaving the cafeteria-style line with our trays loaded, we looked for a place to sit. Several of us sat down at a table occupied by upperclassmen. They had already been there four and a half weeks so they were halfway through the primary flying course. But to hear them talk you would have thought they were seasoned combat veterans. I'm sure they were putting it on for our benefit and it was quite effective. They made certain to speak loud enough so all of us could hear their terrifying dialogue which went something like, "Hey Joe, how'd the aerobatics go this morning?" "Not so good, I spun out of an Immelmann and boy I thought for a while I was going in. If that airplane had done one more turn I was bailing out!"

25

"Yeah, those spins can really get treacherous." All of the newly arrived cadets within earshot were duly impressed. A few were probably wondering what had they gotten themselves into. I was impressed alright but at the same time did have some reservations. I didn't think the primary trainers were really that treacherous and those cadets, four and a half weeks our senior, didn't appear to be any more capable or tougher than the rest of us.

The next morning we were issued our flight gear. We were given heavy sheeplined leather pants, with suspenders to hold them up, a leather jacket and boots. We were also issued a leather helmet and a pair of goggles. My boyhood dreams had become reality. Here I was with my very own helmet and goggles, the symbol of a pilot, issued to me by the United States Army Air Force. These particular helmets were unique to primary flying schools. Small L-shaped metal tubes protruded outward and down from the earpads. Primary flying schools used a very simple but efficient one-way communication system called the "gosport". When two rubber hoses were attached to these tubes, the cadet was equipped with something like a doctor's stethoscope, but instead of listening to heartbeats, the cadet could hear very clearly whatever his instructor had to say.

Next stop was flight operations where we met our instructors. Four cadets were assigned to each instructor. As with most of the war time primary flying schools, the instructors at Grider Field were civilians, but Army Air Corps officers were in charge of the overall operations. Army pilots gave all of the check rides, both the regularly scheduled rides and the much-feared elimination rides.

After the assignments and introductions were completed, we were given our first closeup look at the airplane in which we would be flying for the next nine weeks, the Fairchild PT-19. I thought it was beautiful. The big two-hundred horsepower six cylinder inline inverted Ranger engine, the two open cockpits, and her sleek low wings which were absolutely smooth because they were covered with laminated wood — no ribs showing their edges under fabric, no rivets holding aluminum skin together — just smooth plywood. The tubular steel fuselage was covered with fabric. And there on her sides and wings were the big white stars in the blue circles, the insignia of a United States military aircraft. We were given a short briefing on our parachutes, how they should be inspected, how they should be carried, how they should be worn and when and how they should be used. We were then each given a familiarization ride.

The instructors flew in the rear cockpit and the cadets sat in the front. The PT-19 had no electrical system — no battery, no lights, no radio. The spark plugs were fired by gear-driven magnetos. To start it, the engine had to be cranked by hand. That was the first thing we had to master. A hefty two-handed crank was stowed in a compartment on the left side of the fuselage. We would take it from its compartment, insert it into a hole in the side of the engine cowling and upon the instructor's command, start cranking. As soon as the engine started, we would pull the crank, put it back into the compartment, close the door and climb aboard. We would already be wearing our parachute so all we had to do when we got into the cockpit was fasten the seat belt and slip the rubber hose ends of the gosport onto the metal tubes of our helmet. The instructor personally supervised everything that first time.

His voice came through the gosport, "Just sit back and watch. I'll do the flying." The engine roared and we lifted off. Even behind that windshield there was plenty of wind. It whistled through gaps in my goggles. What a thrill! I was actually in the air. He pointed out landmarks that defined the general flying area. He also showed me where the two auxiliary fields were. Then he showed me a little of the PT-19's capabilities. His voice came through the hoses, "I'll demonstrate a chandelle." All of a sudden, I was jammed down in my seat as the airplane's nose came up and started to swing around the horizon. That was my first introduction to the increased forces of gravity. Most of the instructors tried to not overwhelm the fledglings on those first flights, but more than one cadet came down covered with barf.

The next flight was in earnest, no more joyriding and sightseeing. Everything was done by the numbers including the starting procedure. We had it written down on a card or on white tape stuck on our leather jacket or pants. It was a challenge and response routine just like used on the big jets of today, only this was much shorter and simpler. The cadet standing on the ground beside the airplane with the crank would ask, "Safety belt fastened? Controls free? Brakes set? Gas on fuller tank? Pressure up?" At this point, the man in the cockpit would work the wobble pump until the pressure indicated five pounds per square inch. Next item called was, "Throttle back and cracked? On left mag?" At this point the cadet on the crank would go into action. The engine — and propeller — would start turning and with a cough or two would come to life. The cadet would pull the crank and hold up two fingers, signalling the man in the cockpit to switch to both magnetos. He would then stow the crank in its compartment in the side of the fuselage. The cadets always cranked the engines for their instructors. Later on when the cadets were flying solo, other cadets would do the cranking for their buddies.

We were shown how to taxi, by making S-turns, so we

could see past the nose. We were reminded to not hit the brakes too hard or we'd put it up on its nose. We were shown how to check the mags before takeoff and we were shown how to visually check the sky and the field to make sure we could take off without smashing into another airplane. We were shown how to enter and depart the traffic pattern and most importantly, we began the process of learning to fly.

The Fairchild PT-19 could be termed a low and slow — docile — airplane, but not by the newly arrived cadet. To us it was a powerful brute which had to be conquered. Her specs were not outstanding; max speed: 121 MPH, cruising speed: 100 MPH, stall speed with flaps: 52 MPH, and ceiling 13,000 feet. But she was fully aerobatic and virtually indestructible.

Our first objective was to sufficiently master the bird so that our instructors would let us take it around the field by ourselves. We were taught how to fly it straight and level, how to make coordinated turns — without slipping or sliding. An instrument called the turn and bank indicator, or needle and ball, showed exactly how well you were making the turn. A little black ball inside a curved glass tube would roll to the left or right, depending on which way the airplane was skidding or slipping. If the turn is properly coordinated, the little black ball stays in the middle.

We were also taught how to do stalls, with power on and with power off, straight ahead and in turns. In a good landing, the airplane stalls just as its wheels touch the ground. That's one of the reasons they taught us power-off stalls. Another reason was to teach us how to recognize when the airplane was about to stall and equally important how to recover if the airplane should stall. Power-on stalls were taught because they could occur climbing out after takeoff or on a go around after a missed approach.

Stalls were always practiced at a high enough altitude to allow room for recovery because after the airplane stalls, it must fall to pick up speed in order to start flying again. The instructor would demonstrate the correct technique and then the cadet would try his hand. The instructor would make a couple of clearing turns to make sure that no other airplanes were in the way. Then he would pull the throttle back to idle and at the same time start pulling the stick back. He would use the rudder pedals to keep the nose from swinging to the left or right. As the nose climbed higher and higher, the first signals of the impending stall would appear. The pressures on the control stick and rudder would become very light and the wings would start to shake. As the actual stall occurred, the airplane's nose would fall. To expedite a quick and clean recovery, the procedure was to immediately push the stick forward literally flipping the airplane from its nose-high pre-stall attitude to a straight down dive. As soon as flying speed was attained, the stick would be eased back until the airplane was again flying straight and level. One stall demonstration had an unexpected twist. As the instructor popped the stick forward to initiate the standard recovery, the cadet in the front cockpit went sailing out into the wild blue yonder. He had forgotten to fasten his seat belt, but fortunately he did have his parachute properly fastened. In addition to being the first of our group to "hit the silk", he was presented with a handful of stars for failing to fasten his safety belt. Stars, like demerits, were handed out for any infraction of flying procedures or regulations. Before leaving Primary, each cadet had to pay off for any stars that he received at the rate of twenty-five cents per star.

After about eight hours of dual instruction, of shooting landings, takeoffs, and practicing stalls, we were approaching that long-awaited first milestone. Some cadets soloed in eight hours. Others took longer. If they didn't solo by about twelve hours, they were usually washed out. In spite of all the psychological and coordination tests given to us back at San Antonio, it appeared that there were still a few square pegs among us. You knew whether you were hacking it or not. Nobody had to tell you if you were flying the airplane or if the airplane was flying you.

The routine on the big day was pretty standard. Your instructor would have you do everything. You'd taxi out, take off, fly out to the practice area, do a few stalls, then he'd tell you to go over to Long or Grady, the auxiliary fields, and shoot a landing. After the landing, he'd say, "I've got it," and he'd taxi off to one side of the field and set the brakes. Before climbing out of the cockpit he'd say, into the gosport, something like, "I'm going to get out now so if you think you can get this thing off the ground, around the patch and back again without killing yourself, go to it."

We were introduced to the basics of instrument flying in Link trainers, miserable little boxes that you got into, that balance on top of a little pedestal. We thought they were miserable because we had very little success in making them do what they were supposed to do. Flying the PT-19s in broad daylight was one thing, but sitting inside that little box, looking at all those gauges and trying to fly it over a prescribed course was more than a challenge for our current skill level. Your flight path was precisely plotted, in red ink, on a map on a table nearby. There was no cheating. It was all there in red ink. While trying to do several things at once like talking to the operator over the intercom, planning your course changes and estimating your time en route and times to stations, it was real easy to let your airspeed fall off and stall.

31

In a real airplane you'd have a chance, if you had enough altitude, but not in the Link trainer. It had no wings for air to rush over. If you made a turn too tight or too slow, you'd stall and you'd spin and there was no way to recover, regardless of your altitude. You'd just sit there inside that little box while it went round and round and watch the altimeter unwind. You'd call the operator over the intercom and casually suggest that he turn the thing off. He'd raise the hood and you'd step down and walk over to look at the map, knowing full well what you'd see. The travelling stylus had left its little trail of red ink marking the exact course across the map right up to the point where the spin occurred, where forward travel ended and the little red circles began.

Spinning the PT-19 was a lot more fun than doing it in the Link trainer. You'd pull it up into a stall and just as the stall occurred, you'd slam in full rudder, for whichever way you wanted to spin, right or left. You'd also hold the stick full back. The nose would drop well below the horizon but because the stick was held full back the airplane would remain stalled and continue spinning. You'd count the turns, one, two, three and four. You'd shove in full opposite rudder and push the stick full forward. When the spinning stopped you'd neutralize the rudders and when flying speed had been regained, ease back on the stick and you'd be flying straight and level again. We also learned the basic aerobatic maneuvers, chandelles, slow rolls, barrel rolls, snap rolls, loops and Immelmanns. This was an area where another division began to appear among the cadets. Those wanting to become fighter pilots loved aerobatics, but others were more content to fly straight and level. Some were washed out because of their inability to master the required flying syllabus. Others squeeked through and went on to eventually become copilots on transports and bombers. And a few "bought it" right there in primary.

There were midair collisions but most of the fatal crashes occurred out in the training areas. We had no radios and frequently there were no witnesses. A solo cadet would simply not return after his allotted time was up. Eventually word of the crash would come back. In most cases, the cadet was probably trying some maneuver that got the best of him. One of our classmates dove into a field where a man was picking cotton. They asked him what he saw. He told them he heard this airplane overhead and there it was coming straight down, "Doing about fifteen-hundred miles an hour."

The reason for our heavy leather flying clothes was obvious. The airplanes in which we flew had open cockpits and this was the dead of winter. You could tell how bad the weather was by just looking at the schedule board in flight operations. When the board carried the message, "CADET SOLO FLYING ONLY", you could bet that the weather was lousy. That notice always appeared on the coldest most miserable days. I remember one of those days in particular. All of the instructors were comfortably huddled around the stove while the crazy cadets took to the air. The ground was completely covered with snow. There was a solid overcast and a light snow was falling. There we were, low time student pilots, milling around out there in that terrible weather. You couldn't even make out the horizon. It was just like flying inside of a Ping-Pong ball.

By and large, the relationships between instructors and cadets were good, but I did know of two exceptions. I guess you couldn't have that many men (and boys) involved with each other without having some personality clashes.

One cadet was observed cranking the airplane while his instructor waited in the rear cockpit — the standard procedure. It was a very cold winter day, but the cadet was getting hot. He cranked and cranked but the engine would not start. He was perspiring profusely. He finally took off his big heavy jacket and threw it on the ground and resumed cranking. When he was just about to collapse from exhaustion, a click was heard as the instructor turned on the magneto.

Another story of conflict between cadet and instructor concerned a cadet who already had been around a little. He had been an enlisted man before getting into cadets and possibly thought he knew more than he really did. In any event, they did not get along. Each time he'd screw up a maneuver, the instructor would rapidly shake the stick from side to side. (In a slow airplane like the PT-19 you could do this without anything happening. The ailerons would flap up and down each time the stick was moved but it was so fast the airplane didn't have time to react.) The cadet said the inside of his legs, just above his knees, were black and blue from those stick shakings. Their relationship steadily deteriorated so he decided this would be his last leg beating and his last flight as a cadet. He reached up and eased the rubber hoses, of his gosport, off of his helmet and unzipped his leather pants. (At this point a more detailed explanation of the gosport may be in order. The two rubber hoses, that are attached to the cadet's helmet, are joined at a Y and the single tube goes aft to the instructor's cockpit. A little two-inch funnel is in the end of it and rests in a clip on the inside of the cockpit, just in front of the instructor. It was located so he could speak into the funnel by just leaning forward.) Well, you can probably guess what that soon-to-be-washed-out-cadet did. He peed into the hose and then stuck his end of it out into the slipstream.

After nine weeks at Grider Field and sixty-five hours in PT-19s, we packed up and headed for Basic Flying School.

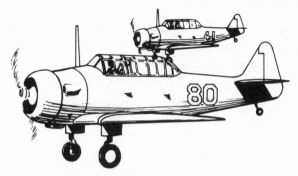

Our first look removed any doubts that Basic Flying School would be a continuation of the relaxed atmosphere which we had enjoyed at primary. This base at Independence, Kansas, was strictly G.I. There were the familiar rows of barracks and everybody was wearing uniforms.

As soon as we were assigned to a flight (barracks) so we could dump our bags, we were sent to the cadet headquarters where we had to individually "report in." Military tradition required a newly assigned officer to personally report to his new commanding officer. As future officers we were required to do the same.

We lined up in single file and waited our turn to "report in." As I neared the head of the line, I could see three officers, each seated at separate desks, handling the chores. It was a fairly large room so the three desks were quite far apart. Although the door remained open, we were supposed to knock before entering. I finally reached the head of the line. A cadet came marching out of the room, meaning that my turn had come. I stepped up to the open door and knocked on the door jamb. A red-faced captain, seated at the middle desk, bellowed, "Drive in here Mister!" I marched in and popped to attention in front of his desk and started to give him a salute when he roared, "Mister! When I say drive in I mean drive in!

You drive back to that door and drive in like you're supposed to!" I marched back to the open doorway, turned around and knocked again. He accepted my performance that time because I at least got the salute off at which time I said, in the required loud voice, "Sir, Aviation Cadet, Wyper, William W., reporting for active duty!" The red in his face grew even deeper as he growled at me, "Mister, I know Pine Bluff is a country club but didn't you consider yourself on active duty?" I replied, "Yes Sir!" He then bellowed, "Mister, when did you wash your belt last?" My khaki web belt was perfectly clean and I knew it, but he had to find fault with something. I replied, "Last month Sir!" His next question thundered throughout the room, "Mister, when did you last wash your face?" I answered, "This morning Sir!" He came right back, "Mister, every time you wash your face, you wash that belt! Do you understand?" Still standing in a rigid brace, I loudly answered, "Yes Sir!" With, "That's all, dismissed." I did an about-face and marched out of the room. But just before I left, I thought I detected a slight smile underneath all of his ferociousness.

The sole function of primary flying school was to get us off the ground and into the air, to start us on our way toward becoming pilots. Basic flying school served additional functions, we were to learn the military way of flying and we were to learn more about becoming officers. That meant everything would be done by the numbers.

We were assigned to our flying instructors, all of whom were first and second lieutenants. I was to soon discover that mine was a tiger, which suited me fine. We were introduced to the airplanes in which we would be flying for the next nine weeks. After the little PT-19s, the BT-14s were really brutes. Our instructors quickly impressed upon us the fact that this was the only basic flying school in the United States which had

North American BT-14s. All of the other basic flying schools were using Vultee BT-13s and BT-15s, known as "Vultee Vibrators". The North American BT-14s had been used at Randolph Field and a few other basic flying schools but because they were no longer made, attrition had taken its toll and these BT-14s at Independence, Kansas, were all that remained. It was made clear to us that we were very lucky to have the opportunity to fly these "last of the breed".

The North American BT-14 looked just like her younger sister, the AT-6, except for one major difference — the BT-14 had fixed landing gear. The main landing gear on AT-6s retracted by swinging toward each other, toward the airplane's centerline. This meant that the gear had to be located far enough apart so they would clear each other when folded up into the wing's center section. Having fixed landing gear, the BT-14 was not confronted with the need for that added width between the main wheels. Consequently, the main gear on the BT-14s was closer together than on the AT-6, and much narrower than the fixed gear on the Vultee Vibrators. This design weakness spelt trouble for the unwary trying to land the BT-14 in any kind of a cross wind, and there was always a cross wind at Independence, Kansas. I'll bet there were more ground loops on that field than any other spot in the United States. Any time you were on frequency you would hear the control tower hollering at some poor cadet who was losing it out there on the runway. You'd hear that anxious voice in the tower shouting, "Give it the throttle! Give it the throttle!" If you happened to be on the ramp or taxiing out, all you had to do was look at the active runway and sure enough, there would be a cloud of dust and a BT-14 grinding out a circle in the dirt beside the runway.

That first familiarization ride in the BT-14 was quite a thrill. As my instructor and I were walking out to our airplane, he said something to another instructor about meeting him somewhere.

He showed me how to conduct the preflight "walk around" inspection of the airplane. It sure seemed big and that radial engine was capable of delivering 450 horsepower — more than twice the power of that Ranger in the PT-19. After I climbed into the rear seat, he showed me how to hook up and use the radio. We no longer wore the helmet and goggles. Instead we used earphones and a microphone which hung on a hook inside the cockpit. In addition to the safety belt, these airplanes were equipped with the standard military type shoulder harness which had two modes controlled by a lever on the left side of the seat. You could have the shoulder harness free-wheeling on its inertia reel so you could lean forward to reach certain things in the cockpit or you could put it in the locked position which held you firmly against the back of your seat. The seats were also adjustable up and down. Except for that first "familiarization" flight, the cadets rode in the front seat, but on that first flight, I was just the passenger, going along for the ride.

With all of the preliminaries out of the way, and clearance from the tower, he advanced the throttle to full forward and the big Pratt & Whitney roared its mightiest as we lifted off and climbed out. I was to find out that my instructor didn't talk much but he was certainly a man of action. Even with my limited experience, I soon realized that I wasn't getting the prescribed indoctrination flight. We were flying along at about two hundred feet above the ground, over some farms and wooded areas. I was enjoying the scenery when all of a sudden the farms that I was looking down at suddenly became the sky. He had just done a slow roll at about two hundred feet. I was pretty sure that wasn't in the familiarization curriculum. But it was a beautiful roll and I enjoyed it. I noticed he kept looking around and pretty soon I saw the reason. Another BT-14 was pulling up beside us. An instructor was flying it with another very young cadet peering out from its rear cockpit. This was the rendezvous they had prearranged. We were still on the deck flying wingtip to wingtip when my instructor did something that really impressed me. He raised our right wing and eased it over on top of their left wing and then gently laid our wing tip down on theirs. I was sure that maneuver was not in the book. We soon split off and eventually returned to the field. As we walked back to the operations room, he didn't make any reference to the demonstration that I had just witnessed and I didn't say anything either.

My next flight was in the front seat, at which time my instructor informed me that I would not see the airspeed indicator until I soloed. It was completely covered with masking tape. This made things difficult for a while but eventually I got the feel of it. In those first few hours it was tough. He'd holler at me over the intercom that I was going too fast or that I was going too slow. How was I to know — I couldn't see the airspeed indicator. Apparently I satisfied him though because after about four hours of takeoffs, stalls and landings, he climbed up on the wing and reached into my cockpit and pulled the tape off of the airspeed indicator and told me to have at it.

Doing aerobatics in the BT-14 was a lot more gratifying than in the PT-19. This was a heavier and more powerful airplane. All of the standard aerobatic maneuvers were demonstrated and then we were given solo time in which to practice and perfect them. I never will forget my first solo attempts at doing Immelmanns.

I was in my assigned practice area, one of the many squares marked off on the area map. I was at about seven or eight thousand feet, high enough to either recover from an accidental spin or to bail out in case the recovery didn't work. I did the two ninety-degree clearing turns, to make sure no one else was trying to share the same chunk of sky. Then I lowered the nose to pick up some added speed. I pulled back on the stick. With about four Gs (four times gravity) pushing me down in the seat the BT-14 came up into the first half of a loop. As the airplane approached the top and started over on its back, the normal procedure was to tilt your head back so you could see the horizon come into view. As the nose starts down toward the horizon, you'd do a half roll to either the left or right bringing the airplane right side up again, and completing the Immelmann. Well, I was doing everything by the book, I thought, but just as I reached the top, the airplane did the half roll all by itself. Even though I had a firm grip on the stick, I could feel it move as the airplane rolled from inverted to right side up — completing the Immelmann for me. I was mystified. I thought I must have done something wrong, but what? I didn't know. So I tried another one. I dived down, picked up speed, pulled up into the half loop and just as I came over the top inverted, damned if the airplane didn't roll out again probably better than I could have done it. Because of the stick forces that I felt during those roll outs, I thought there must be some wise guy in my back seat. I actually unfastened my harness and seat belt and raised up out of my seat to get a better view into the rear cockpit. It was empty. My solo period was about up, but I tried one more and darned if it didn't do the same thing. I never said anything about that to my instructor or fellow cadets for fear they would think I was nuts, but after gaining more flying experience, I realized that I had been encountering stalls at the top of those loops and the aerodynamic characteristics of the airplane at that particular speed and altitude, caused it to snap, giving me a rather smart-looking conclusion to my Immelmanns.

Basic Flying School

Life in Basic Flying School wasn't all in the air. This was strictly a military operation and we were subjected to numerous hours of ground school, PT, marching close order drill, gigs and tours. We also had morning roll call. Kansas in the dead of winter is not the most pleasant spot and standing out on a road in the pitch-blackness of predawn was probably the least desirable of all. They didn't really take roll call out there on the road but they did check the barracks while the formation was held on the road. And pity any poor cadet found in the barracks during that time. After a few sessions of standing out there on that road in the black of night shivering in the cold, something became apparent. We'd just fall into the standard formation on the side of the street, four long lines of cadets facing the officer on the other side. There was no set formation. You'd just stumble into a line and stand there beside the next man. No roll call was taken. You'd just stand there while they went through the ritual. I guess it had to be long enough to allow time for the tactical officers to go stomping through the barracks. One by one, each cadet lieutenant would report for his flight, then the cadet captains would do an about-face and report, "Squadron one, all present and accounted for Sir!" "Squadron two, all present and accounted for Sir!" and the litany continued on down the long line of cadets silently standing there in the dark. The cadet commandant would then do an about-face, click his heels, salute the poor commissioned officer, unlucky enough to draw that morning duty, and shout, "Sir! All present and accounted for!" The commissioned officer would complete the ritual by saying, "Dismiss your troops." The cadet commandant would then do another about-face, to face the troops, click his heels again and shout at the top of his lungs, "Fall out!" The shivering cadets would then jog back to their respective barracks and line up in the latrines for their turn at a sink so

41

they could shave before going to breakfast. Well, one morning as I was running out of the barracks on my way to roll call, as I passed the latrine, I noticed that the lights were turned off in the shower room. After all, nobody could be taking showers so it was logical that the lights would be off. While standing out there on the road that morning, a devious thought crossed my mind, a thought which I would transform into action the following day.

The next morning as the cadets were rushing out of the barracks, I picked up my shaving kit and instead of heading out the door, I turned into the latrine and stepped into the dark shower room. To my surprise, I soon discovered that I was not alone. As my eyes adjusted to the darkness, I could see silhouettes of about five or six fellow cadets standing there against the wall. We heard the barrack door swing open and could hear the tac officer and his stooges, the accompanying cadet officers who would write down the names of anyone caught in the barracks. They went stomping through the barracks and out the door at the other end. Pretty soon we heard the thunder of footsteps pounding down the wooden walkways to the barracks. That was our signal to step out of the shower room and up to a wash basin to start shaving. That was pretty neat. Not only did we escape the misery of standing out in the cold, we also were the first to get shaved. But our pleasures were short lived. We weren't really fooling our cadet officer so it was no big surprise when three of our names appeared on the bulletin board ordering us to reply by endorsement as to why we missed morning roll call on "14 November". It did seem odd though that they singled out one specific date when we in fact had missed it every morning. My two fellow offenders hand-wrote their replies, giving some feeble excuses why they weren't there. I thought I'd try something different. I went to the ground school library and looked up the correct form for a formal military letter. Then I went to the orderly room and asked to use one of their typewriters for a few minutes. My letter went something like:

TO: The Commandant of Cadets

SUBJECT: Missing morning roll call on 14 November

Sir, I demand an explanation why I was marked absent from roll call on the morning of 14 November, because no roll call was taken and there was no set element formation.

A/C Wyper, William W.

Within minutes after my letter reached the commandant of cadets, I was summoned by special messenger to report immediately. I sort of expected a prompt response.

I knocked on his door. He said come in. I marched up to his desk, popped to attention, saluted and said, "Sir, Aviation Cadet Wyper, William W., reporting as ordered." He had my letter in his hands. He put on a good act. He looked really fierce. He growled, "Mister! You are a cadet! I am a captain! You do not demand explanations from me!! Do you understand that?" Standing in a stiff brace, I answered, "Yes Sir!" He repeated, "Are you sure you understand that?" Again, I replied, "Yes Sir!" He then said, "That's all. Dismissed." I saluted, did an about-face and left. I knew that he appreciated my ingenuity because he did not ask me if I was at that formation. If he had asked, I would have had to have said no. The other two offenders were awarded a couple of hours walking tours for their feeble excuses, which were in fact lies. Mine wasn't.

The ramp at Independence, Kansas, held row after row of BT-14s and one big olive drab A-17, which occupied the parking spot in front of flight operations headquarters. The A-17 was somewhat of a rarity in the Army Air Corps because it was really a Navy airplane known as the Curtiss Helldiver, SB2C. I asked my instructor why that airplane was based at this Basic Flying School. He explained that Kansas was a dry state and permitted no liquor within its boundaries. This field was considered federal property and therefore was exempt from local state laws. No officer's club anywhere in the world would be without booze and that included Independence, Kansas. The big olive drab Helldiver was used to fly in the booze.

Every four and a half weeks, one class left and a new class arrived. Each cadet had nine weeks in which to complete the required number of flying hours covering the specific objectives. When flying days were lost due to bad weather, catching up was sometimes a problem. Being there through the worst part of the winter, we were confronted with the problem of catching up. At one point of our basic flight training, we were required to log six night takeoffs and landings. With only a few nights available, it was somewhat of a challenge to devise a method by which the entire class could get in their required six night takeoffs and landings. But they had a method designed to accomplish all objectives. Virtually all of the airplanes would take off into the night sky. Each cadet would fly out to his specified zone where he would tool around to await his call to enter a pattern. The patterns were really hairy. They would have four or five levels of patterns and each level would have as many as six airplanes. The last twenty or so airplanes to take off would remain in the patterns at different levels. Of that group, the first six to take off would be ordered to climb, in the pattern, to 4,000 feet. (The pattern was an invisible rectangle, in plan view, with one of its long sides right over the runway. The short side on the upwind end of the runway is called the crosswind leg. The other long side, parallel to the runway, is called the downwind leg, and the other short side, at the downwind end of the runway, is called the base leg.) The next six airplanes would be told to climb, after takeoff, in the pattern to 3,000 feet. The next six cadets would be assigned 2,000 feet and the last six airplanes off the ground would remain in the landing pattern at 1,000 feet. By the time the last cadet had taken off, the first one in his group of six would be coming in for his first landing. They had floodlights beside the threshold of the runway so the instructors, in the mobile control unit, could read the numbers on the sides of the airplanes. After each cadet landed, he would receive a command over his radio from the mobile control. Until all six landings had been accomplished, the radio command was usually, "O.K. number so and so, give it the gun and go around again." But if a cadet was really making bad landings he would be called in before he attempted any more. If six landings were the number required for that particular night, each cadet would be called off the runway. after his sixth landing. After all of the airplanes in the lowest pattern had made their final landings and taxied off the runway, the next level, the group orbiting at 2,000 feet, would be called down to the 1,000 foot level so they could start making their landings and takeoffs. When that entire group had arrived at the 1,000 foot level, the group orbiting at 3,000 feet would be called down to the 2,000 foot level and the group at 4,000 feet would be called down to 3,000. Then another group of cadets, who were out flying around in their assigned areas, would be called in to start orbiting the pattern at 4,000. Well, as you can imagine, things didn't always go as smoothly as planned. Those night operations at Independence, Kansas, were becoming notorious because of their high number of midair collisions. Word spread to the nearby bases, at Coffeyville, Kansas and Bartlesville, Oklahoma, about the fireballs dropping out of the night sky at Independence. We did have more than our share of midairs. In fact it became so serious that the base commander called a special meeting in the base theater. All of the cadets were in attendance, both upper and lower class. The base commander walked out on the stage. Someone shouted the usual "Tenhut!" Everybody popped to attention. After the customary "At ease, be seated," the colonel delivered his message. I'll never forget his very brief speech. He said, "As you all know, we have had an exceedingly high number of airplane accidents. As you also know, this is the last remaining basic flying school in the United States to use the North American BT-14. There are no more North American BT-14s. Now I don't give a damn if you men want to kill yourselves but we can't afford to lose any more of our BT-14s. From now on, I expect every one of you to keep your heads out. There will be no more accidents. That's an order!" That short speech was a far cry from Hollywood's treatment of a similar situation in the movie version of "Winged Victory" which came out toward the end of World War II. One sequence depicted a night flying accident at a basic flying school. In the screen version, the base commander was portrayed as a kindly colonel who came to the cadet's quarters to personally console the cadet, whose buddy had just been killed. We, who had been there, knew the way it really was.

Another objective to be accomplished in basic flying school was to master the art of cross-country navigation. Cadets flew solo on the cross-countries and they were dispatched at two-minute intervals so they had to do their own navigation, not just follow the airplane ahead. Certain rules prevailed on the cross-country flights, one of which was absolutely no aerobatics. And just to assure that the rules were obeyed, instructors were out there in other BT-14s patrolling the course. One senior instructor, a captain, came into our operations and told us what he had just encountered that morning while patrolling one leg of the cross-country. He said that he was cruising along, parallel to the course, when he noticed a BT-14 some distance to his right. The captain said that he then heard a radio call, "Hey there, BT over there on my left. If you hear me do a slow roll." The captain said that in accordance with the request, he did a slow roll. Then another message came over the radio from the cadet off the captain's right, "That was a pretty good roll. Now watch me do a square loop." The captain said, "He did a pretty darn good square loop, but that was a violation of the rules so I moved in and got his number. Now one particular aviation cadet is in big trouble." He was punished but because he did such a good square loop, they just couldn't wash him out.

My last cross-country in basic flying school turned out to be a real fiasco. We were scheduled to fly a triangular course, legs of which were about one hundred miles long. At the end of the first leg, we were to check in by radio with an instructor who would be using the radio of his BT parked on the ground. It was a little auxiliary landing field. The second checkpoint was simply a dot on the map — a very small community — just a spot where two roads came together. We were to be dispatched at the usual two-minute intervals. The cadet who was scheduled to take off right ahead of me came over and said, "Hey Wyper, I'll circle around and wait for you north of the field and we can fly the cross-country together." Being a straight arrow I really didn't want to, but contrary to my better judgement, I agreed.

We taxied out to the south end of the runway and waited our turn to be dispatched. The tower told him to take off, then two minutes later, told me to take off. I climbed out right on course and there at about 4,000 feet was my old buddy circling around. He pulled in on my wing and we flew on to the first checkpoint. As we neared the call-in point, I gave him the sign that I would do a 360-degree turn to give us a little spacing before we flew over that instructor stationed on the ground. He nodded O.K. and I peeled off to make one circle. I heard him call in and I heard the acknowledgement from the instructor on the ground. As I flew over the parked BT-14, I called in but got no answer. I tried again, then I realized that I wasn't transmitting. I could hear them, but they couldn't hear me. So I circled around and dropped down to about a hundred feet and flew past the parked airplane so the instructor could read my number. I wiggled my wings to signal that I could not transmit. He responded by saying, "Number so and so, if you hear me but can't transmit, wiggle your wings again." I did. He then said, "Roger, number so-and-so, proceed on course." I was already on course climbing back to our assigned altitude. It wasn't long before I came upon my old buddy circling around waiting for me. This time I joined up on his wing. I had navigated on the first leg so I'd let him take over on the second leg. That proved to be a mistake.

We sat there grinding along looking at each other for what seemed to be an awful long time. I couldn't look at my map because my complete attention was required to keep in position on his wing. He hadn't been paying much attention to his map but finally it came out and I could see that he was really studying it. He'd look at the map, then down at the ground, then at the map again. He looked over at me and gestured with his hands to show that he didn't know where we were. I had suspected as much. He pointed and gestured to ask me if I knew where we were. I didn't. If a cadet is going to get lost on a cross-country, the one thing he doesn't want is to be lost in the company of another cadet. We both knew that so with mutual signals we split up. He made a 180-degree turn and I kept going straight ahead. Now no longer in formation, I could devote full time to my map. This cross-country flight was supposed to be an exercise in dead reckoning. We were expected to use ground checkpoints to calculate wind drift and fly against elapsed time. My expert navigator apparently used neither on that second leg so there I was somewhere, but I didn't know where, over the middle of Kansas. We had been instructed in a procedure that was authorized in the event that we became completely lost. It was called "shooting a station". You were to fly along until you found a railroad track. Then you were to fly above the railroad track until you came upon a station. All railroad stations had their names on the ends of the station house so they could be read by approaching trains. The idea was to fly along the track low enough to read the name on the first station you came to. Then you would know where you were. Pretty soon I heard my buddy call the Independence control tower and tell them he had just flown over the railroad station at Piedmont. They told him to stand by for a heading back to the field. After a brief pause, the tower called him back and gave him the heading. Being an eager beaver and maybe a little stupid, I was still trying to find that second checkpoint. But first I figured I'd better find out where I was so I settled down on a railroad track to find me a station. Pretty soon one came into view. As I flashed past, the name was very distinct — El Dorado. I pulled up to a safe altitude so I could consult my map. I concentrated my search for El Dorado in the area of the map where I thought I was, but I couldn't find it. Then, all of a sudden there it was right in the white border on the edge of my sectional chart. One more mile to the west and it wouldn't even have been on my map. Now I at least knew where I was. In fact it would have been real easy to pick up a course directly back to Independence, but dummy me, I wanted to go back and find that second checkpoint. I plotted a course to it from El Dorado and set off in that direction. After a while it dawned on me that

I couldn't stay up there much longer. Both tanks were getting very low. That meant one thing. I would have to find a spot to put it down. My left tank was showing empty and the right was not far from it. I could see what appeared to be a town on the horizon so I headed in that direction. I had to find an airport to land. I saw a railroad track leading in that direction so I again dropped down to follow the "iron beam" to the first station house, which happened to be right in the heart of town. The station was nice and big and so was its sign — Emporia. I pulled up, took a quick look at my map and found the symbol of an airport just north of town. I banked 90 degrees to the left and started slowing down. It was a little dirt field with some Piper Cubs. I saw no other traffic in the way so I glided in and landed. I taxied up to the hangar and shut it down. I was greeted like Lindbergh at Le Bourget, but my spirit could not have been lower. They showed me where the telephone was so I went over to make the dreaded call. I told them where I was and that I would need some gas in order to fly back to Independence. The little Cub operation didn't have the right octane gas for the Pratt & Whitney.

Those long hours that I waited gave me more than enough time to think about how not to fly a simple cross-country. About four hours later, a BT-14 appeared overhead and after a couple of low passes, came in and landed. Twenty gallons of gas were transferred to my airplane and we took off for the flight home. Normally I loved flying and especially formation but there was no joy in that flight back to Independence because of what waited for me upon my arrival. As soon as I landed and parked the airplane, I headed for my squadron commander's office to report my stupidity.

He was an old-time pilot with an S on his wings, meaning that he was a Service Pilot. They were civilian pilots who for one reason or another could not fully qualify as regular military pilots. It was evident what his problem was. He wore a hearing aid. His hearing had no doubt been impaired by thousands of hours of sitting in open cockpits behind thundering exhaust stacks.

I was stammering and stuttering, trying to explain why I had goofed up. I referred to things like wind drift and compass deviation, and all the time failing to mention the fact that another cadet had helped to get me lost. After so much of my B.S., he said, "You know, there's not a pilot flying who hasn't gotten lost. All pilots experience it at one time or another. You just had yours. Now, give yourself five stars." At twenty-five cents per star, that cost me a dollar and a quarter.

As our nine weeks of basic flying school were drawing to a close, we, of the graduating class, were apprised of a problem. We were called to the messhall to hear one of the administrative officers. He said, "Gentlemen, you are about to leave Basic and go on to Advance Flying School, but we seem to have a slight problem. You may recall a couple of weeks ago you were asked to state your preference for either single engine advance or multi-engine. Well we have nearly two hundred more requests for single engine advance than there are openings. All of you can't be fighter pilots. That's why we've called you here today to tell you this and to suggest that any of you who had requested single engine, who would just as soon go to multi-engine, to please give us your names." The more I thought about this dilemma, the more worried I became, because knowing how the military did things I was sure they would take their single-engine quota alphabetically, and completely fill it long before reaching the W's. I had to do something so I came up with an idea that was at least worth trying.

I went to the orderly room and asked to see whoever was handling the lists for single engine advance. The sergeant said he was and asked what he could do for me. I asked him if it would be possible to revise some of the information given earlier. He got out the list and located my name. I said that I would like to change my height from six feet to five feet eleven inches and that I would like to change my weight from 170 to 160. This was really splitting hairs but a myth prevailed that smaller pilots had a better chance of getting picked for fighters than the larger taller men. At this point I would try anything. The sergeant looked at me and smilingly said O.K. As I was leaving, I thought I saw him put a mark of some kind by my name.

My earlier fears were well-founded because they did exactly what I thought they might. The cadet quota for single engine advance apparently had been filled alphabetically because no name starting with letters beyond R was on that list except one, Wyper, William W.

About twice as many cadets went off to multi-engine. That seemed logical because there were a lot of bombers and transports and more were being built and each one needed two pilots. Many of the cadets always wanted to go to multi-engine but there were others like myself who had their hearts set on becoming fighter pilots. For those aspiring young tigers whose names started with S, T, U, V, W, X, Y and Z, it was a sad day.

Everybody in my barracks had names that started with W, X, Y or Z, so when they shipped out for multi-engine advance flying school one day before the group for single engine advance was to leave, only one man was left. That last night in Independence, alone in that big empty barrack, my thoughts were about flying and what lay ahead. Tomorrow I would be heading for a place that I had never even heard of before seeing it typed on my orders, but it sure sounded like the place to fly AT-6s — Eagle Pass, Texas.

Eagle Pass, Texas, is located right on the Rio Grande, about one hundred miles north of Laredo. On the other side of the Rio Grande is Mexico and some pretty rugged country.

The base looked no different than many others with its hastily built single story tar paper barracks. But on the flight line were the beautiful single engine advance trainers, the North American AT-6s.

Arriving at advance generated a special anxiety because we were getting close to the end of our training. This would be our last assignment as cadets. We would leave here with silver wings and gold bars, or if fate dealt a bad hand, leave as a former cadet and new buck private, and according to proven statistics, a very few would leave in boxes.

After the usual assignment to quarters, moving in, drawing ground school books, and taking another six-four flight physical, we finally made it to the flight line to meet our

53

new instructors. Six cadets were assigned to each instructor. Most of our flying would be solo so each instructor could easily handle that number of students. After all of the introductions and handshakes we were shown the AT-6. Although reminiscent of the BT-14, the AT-6 had a 600 horsepower Pratt & Whitney, retractable landing gear, and for our gunnery missions, would carry a forward-firing fixed 30-caliber machine gun. I had an immediate edge over the other five cadets because they came from basic flying schools which had the Vultee Vibrators. Flying the AT-6 was very similar to flying her older sister the BT-14. The cadets who had been flying the virtually foolproof Vultee Vibrators found the AT-6 to be a bit of a challenge during those first few hours. But it wasn't long before everybody soloed and it wasn't much longer before most of us had mastered all of the basic maneuvers that the T-6 was capable of performing. The procedure was to have periodic rather short flights with our instructor and many more solo flights giving us time to practice the newly learned maneuvers. One item in our curriculum was to log twelve solo spins. I knew for a fact that many of the cadets did those spins only on their log sheets with their Parker pens, but being real Gung Ho I did everything by the book. I figured that would make me a better pilot and might very well save my life someday in a combat situation.

On previous solo flights I had already accomplished six of my solo spins so one afternoon when I was assigned an airplane for an hour and a half, I figured among other maneuvers that I would practice, I'd knock off at least three more spins.

With parachute over my shoulder, I walked along the ramp looking for my assigned airplane. I finally found it parked way down at the far end of the ramp. I walked around it in the customary fashion. It appeared to be all in one piece.

Before every solo flight we were supposed to always check the back seat to make sure that the shoulder harness and seat belt were fastened and that the rear canopy was closed and locked. So as I climbed onto the wing, I glanced at the rear canopy and looked at the seat. The harness was secured and the canopy was closed and locked. I climbed into the front cockpit, fastened my harness, plugged in my earphones, looked at the log book, then fired it up, called the tower and taxied out to take off.

Upon reaching ten thousand feet I set about to do my first spin for the day. I made the standard clearing turns, one ninety-degree turn to the right and one ninety-degree turn to the left. No other airplanes were in sight. I eased the throttle back while pulling back on the stick to bring the nose high above the horizon. Just as it stalled, I jammed in full left rudder. She dropped off into a good left spin. I counted the turns, one, two, three, four, and now to recover. I shoved in full right rudder and pushed the stick forward and held them waiting for the spin to stop. It usually made one more turn before stopping but this time it just didn't want to stop spinning. It made at least three more turns before slowing down. I was really starting to get sweaty palms. I neutralized the rudders and waited for enough airspeed to pull out. I let the airspeed build up to 180 miles per hour and then very gently hauled it back to level flight. I had been exposed to secondary stalls which occur when you horse the stick back too quickly during those pull outs. Instead of returning to level flight, the airplane violently shakes and goes immediately into a tighter spin. With the trouble I had getting it out of that first spin, I sure didn't want a secondary stall and a tighter spin.

As I climbed back up to regain all of my lost altitude, I had time to think, to try to figure out what went wrong with that spin recovery. I had done everything the same way I always did but this bird didn't want to stop spinning. I figured I had not done something right. So once more, the two clearing turns, then up and into it, one turn, two, three, four and now full opposite rudder and stick forward, five, six, seven and finally it slowed down and stopped rotating. That was terrible. I had to be doing something wrong. I climbed back up to twelve thousand feet and tried one more time. My recovery that time was no better. It made three more full turns before I could get it stopped. Well, that was enough for one day anyway. At least I did my three spins, as bad as they were. After parking the airplane, as I was climbing down off of the wing, I saw the large red placard on the side of the fuselage right in front of the horizontal stabilizer. How could I have missed it before? NO AEROBATIC MANEUVERS WHEN WINCH IS INSTALLED. I leaped back onto the wing and looked into the rear cockpit and behind the seat was a large winch loaded with stainless steel cable. This AT-6 was used to tow the gunnery targets. I was lucky to be alive.

Inverted spins were not authorized maneuvers in any of our training airplanes, but with obliging instructors, I had been allowed to try one in Primary, one in Basic and one in Advance. At least in those three types of airplanes it was fairly easy. To enter the inverted spins, I'd chop the throttle and pull the nose up while doing a half roll to get inverted. Just as it stalled, I'd push in one rudder all the way. The stick would already be full forward to keep the nose up while inverted. The forces during inverted spins tried to throw you out of the cockpit. It required tremendous effort, while hanging in your harness, to keep that rudder pedal pushed in all the way and to hold the stick full forward. But the recovery was extremely simple. All you had to do was relax. The depressed rudder pedal and stick would both return to their neutral positions. The nose would fall, putting the airplane into a straight down dive. Airspeed was quickly regained so all you had to do was ease back on the stick to bring the airplane back up to straight and level flight.

Another objective in advance flying school was to give us the ability to take off and fly with no visual reference outside of the cockpit. Since our first introduction to the Link Trainer back in Primary, we had developed enough proficiency to keep it from stalling and spinning. We had logged a number of hours in the Link Trainer and we also were flying under the hood in the rear seat of AT-6s. We even made takeoffs while under the hood. The instructor, riding in the front seat, would line up the airplane on the runway's centerline and then relinquish the controls to the cadet under the hood in the back seat. While intently watching the directional gyro, and airspeed, we would advance the throttle to full power. As the airspeed started to increase, we'd be furiously working the rudder pedals and very gently easing the stick forward, just enough to get the tail up, and then slightly back again to lift off. At this point, a lot more instruments required watching; needle and ball, artificial horizon, rate of climb and altimeter, in addition of course to the airspeed and directional gyro, which we were already watching. It was a sweaty three-ring circus under that hood. After the under-the-hood checkout by our instructors, we got several more hours of practice hood time on buddy rides. These were the only flights in single engine advance when two cadets flew together in the same airplane.

When a cadet had an airplane assigned to him for an instrument flight, he would get one of his buddies, who wasn't scheduled for a flight during that particular period, to fly with him in the front seat. His function would be to act as an observer, to make sure they didn't run into any other airplanes and of course the ground. The prescribed procedure was for the man in the front seat to make the takeoff and landing. Throughout the rest of the flight the cadet in the rear seat was supposed to be under the hood practicing his instrument flying. The first part of the flights was pretty conventional. It was usually the last portion of the flights when the rules got broken. After about a half hour or so of sweating "on the gauges", the hood would invariably be opened and the demonstration would begin. This was the only time when two cadets could show each other how skillful they were in aerobatics. Most of us got away with it but one tragic incident did occur.

The cadet in the rear seat decided that he had had enough instrument flying for that day so he unhooked the hood and pushed it back out of his way. He was ready for a little competitive aerobatics. The airplane peeled off and headed for the deck. The cadet in the rear seat settled back to see what his buddy in the front seat was going to do. It was later deduced that the cadet in the front seat was also relaxing and anticipating a demonstration by his buddy in the rear seat. Each man thought the other was flying the airplane. The shallow descent continued on down to within a few feet of the ground. The airplane seemed to level out as it got close to the ground further substantiating each man's belief that the other man was on the controls. The sagebrush of Southwestern Texas was flashing by at 180 miles per hour. Then it happened.

In spite of the crash and ensuing fire, the cadet in the rear seat was able to get out. But just as soon as he caught his breath, he went back and tried desperately to get his buddy out of the burning airplane. His valiant efforts were to no avail. One cadet died in the accident and the other was severely burned.

A policy prevailed throughout our training that whenever a cadet was killed, one of his classmates would be selected to accompany the body back to the deceased's home town. In most cases they picked a cadet who was either from the same home town or was at least from the same general area. That way the escorting cadet would get a few hours to visit with his folks or maybe see his hometown sweetheart.

We had been introduced to night flying back in basic flying school but that was mostly just getting used to being up there in the dark. We went out into the night and did a few maneuvers, then came back to the field and concentrated on landings and takeoffs. In advance they assumed that we knew how to fly the airplane, even at night, so the emphasis was on night cross-country navigation. All of the flights were solo. But, before we undertook any of these night flights, we were apprised of yet another rule. Being as how the AT-6 had only one engine, there was a hard and fast rule regarding engine failure at night. If your engine ever stopped at night, and you could not safely glide down and land on a lit runway, the order was: you must bail out. No ifs ands or buts. That was the rule. Their reasoning was that if you tried to put the airplane down somewhere other than on a lit runway, you'd smash up the airplane and kill yourself. The night bail out rule would cut their losses. They would lose the airplane but not the pilot. Well, it seems that rules have a way of getting broken.

One night a cadet was flying along on one leg of his cross-country when his engine quit. Presumably he did the immediate checks, switched fuel tanks, turned on the auxiliary fuel pump, etc., but his engine was dead. Beneath him in the partial moonlight he could see a paved highway. He just couldn't bring himself to abandon a perfectly good airplane when it seemed obvious to him that he could make a normal landing on that road. In any event, gravity was exercising another rule on his two-and-a-half-ton instant glider so the decision had been made. He reached down and placed his gear handle in the down position. The landing gear would fall down and lock into place even without the engine-driven hydraulic pressure. He could feel the gear clunk down into place. He could see, reflecting in the moonlight, the long straight road extending out ahead of him. He glided on down and made a very good landing. During his entire descent he never saw any headlights and that same luck remained on his side during the landing. After he came to a stop, there wasn't anything more that he could do. He had already notified Eagle Pass of his plight the instant that his engine quit. He got off the required mayday message. They would be on their way to search the general area. Although the moonlight was adequate to see the shiny road from the air, everything now looked mighty dark so he figured he'd better stay with his airplane and try to prevent any cars, trucks or whatever might come along from hitting the parked airplane.

As the first rays of morning light penetrated the area, he was aghast over what he saw. Oil derricks lined both sides of the narrow two-lane road upon which sat his AT-6 with its wingtips extending to both edges. If he had banked to either left or right, prior to touchdown, he would have been wiped out. He did save the airplane but he also violated a standing order. A regulation which, after seeing those oil wells, he could better understand its reasoning.

Those solo night cross-country flights were a thrilling experience. All of our instruments had radium dials which glowed under the little fluorescent spotlights. The amount of glow was controlled by rheostats for the little fluorescent lights. You'd sit up there in the black of night behind that thundering 600 HP Pratt & Whitney with your attention divided between those softly glowing instruments and the sleeping Texas countryside far below. Our system of navigation was basically dead reckoning. We would plot the prescribed course on our map and measure the distances which we then converted to time. We would fly out the elapsed times while looking for checkpoints on the ground. Each checkpoint was usually a town of some size so there would be enough lights for us to find and identify it. Fortunately there weren't many big towns in our part of Texas so there wasn't much confusion in identifying the right cluster of lights. It was fun and gratifying to be able to find your way through the night sky to towns hundreds of miles away and back again to your home base. But, one night a few less daring cadets decided to forego the challenge.

As with all cadet solo cross-country flights, the cadets were dispatched with at least a three-minute interval between each takeoff. One night after all the cadets had been dispatched, a strange situation became apparent. Because of the total distance to be flown and the number of airplanes on the course, it would be at least an hour and a half before the first AT-6s would be arriving back and landing. Yet there were distinct sounds of AT-6s flying around over the field. This was indeed a curious situation. It was too dark to see them and to make it even more bizarre, they were flying around up there with all of their lights turned off. They should be showing their navigation lights, a green light on their right wingtip, a red one on their left wingtip and a white one on their tail. Those airplanes were flying around up there in the dark with their lights turned off and to make it absolutely terrifying, you could tell by the sounds of their engines that they were not flying together in any organized fashion. They were flying around in circles but it sounded like every man was on his own. Whoever they were up there in those AT-6s, they were truly playing Russian roulette. At any minute you expected to see a big fireball and at least two AT-6s come falling out of that night sky, but somehow they lucked out.

By carefully monitoring the returning aircraft, the officers in charge were able to identify the orbiting aircraft. They would see their navigation lights come on as they let down to enter the traffic pattern to land. It turned out they were four of the Brazilian cadets who were taking their advance flight training at Eagle Pass. The cross-country that night was a triangular course to Del Rio and San Antonio and back to Eagle Pass. There were no call-in checkpoints en route so those Brazilian cadets thought they would play it safe and not run the risk of venturing that far away and possibly getting lost. Instead, they simply turned off their lights and circled around over the field until the required amount of time elapsed. Then they came down and landed.

Aerial markmanship was the part of our advance training that made us think that maybe we really were on our way toward becoming fighter pilots. But if blasting enemy aircraft out of hostile skies was our goal, learning the sport of skeet shooting seemed like a strange beginning. Their rationale was that skeet shooting trained our eyes and our reflexes to lead and hit fast moving targets at widely varying angles of deflection. Anyway it was fun and most of us became expert skeet shooters but only by memorizing the amount of lead required to hit the little clay pigeons from each of the different stations. The maximum amount of lead was three feet when the bird's path was at ninety degrees to our position. That was full deflection. Some of the other shots were nearly head-on or trailing. Each round of skeet consisted of twenty-five clay pigeons. We would regularly hit twenty-three and twenty-four out of the twenty-five. The real fun came though when we started shooting at aerial targets with the 30-caliber machine gun mounted in the nose of our AT-6.

There would be from four to six cadets on each gunnery mission, all shooting at the same target. Individual scorekeeping was possible because the bullets for each airplane were painted a different color. Before loading the guns, the armorers would roll up the belts of ammo on a table with the bullets pointing up. They would then drag a wide paint brush across the tips, using a different color of paint for each airplane. When counting hits in the target after the mission, each bullet hole would be ringed with its own identifying color.

We would fly a well-spaced follow-the-leader rectangular pattern about a thousand feet above the airplane towing the target. As the AT-6, towing the target, came toward us we would each in turn make a firing pass at the target. We would peel out of the rectangular pattern, making a diving turn to approach the target at a full ninety degree deflection, then steepen the bank to move the pipper of our sight ahead of the target, quickly glance down to make sure the ball in the turn and bank indicator was centered, then squeeze the trigger sending a volley of bullets hopefully into the target. Because of the fast rate of closure we'd only have a couple of seconds to fire, then we'd have to make a fast descending bank to keep from smashing into the target or the tow cable. We'd slide underneath the target and climb back up on the other side, back into the rectangular pattern and wait for our next turn.

After each gunnery mission, we'd anxiously wait for the target to be brought back to the ramp so our hits could be counted. The airplane towing the target would fly over the field and release the target. A truck would pick it up and bring it to the ramp where it would be spread out for everyone's scrutiny. It was made of very heavy metal screen-type material and was supposed to present about the same profile area as an airplane. They were called banner targets because they trailed through the sky at the end of the cable like a banner. The bottom edge was weighted to keep its vertical position. No matter how many of your hits were found and counted, you always felt that there should have been more.

Each day was divided between ground school, PT and flying. Half of the cadets would fly in the morning and go to ground school and physical training in the afternoon. The other half would do the opposite. During the half-day on the flight line, every cadet would usually get in at least one flight. Each instructor had two or three airplanes for his cadets. He would assign them as he saw fit. The instructors would frequently use one for dual and assign the other airplane or airplanes to their cadets for individual periods of solo flying. While waiting for our turns to fly, there was always plenty of studying to do so the time went pretty fast. One day all six of us flew together. It was a very rare and unwelcomed occasion.

When not briefing us or coordinating our flights, the instructors remained in their own ready room adjacent to the room where the cadets gathered before, after and while waiting their turns to fly. Every day when we arrived at the flight line we would gather in little groups and wait for our respective instructors like chicks waiting for their mother hen. One afternoon, our instructor came out from the instructor's room and walked over to our little group and dropped the bomb on us.

Unlike many of the other more gregarious second lieutenants, our instructor was a low-key quiet gentleman, but a good instructor who had our deepest respect. He was never a bundle of laughs but that day, even his hello conveyed a somber and tense mood. He said, "The Air Inspector is going to give us a formation check ride. Here are your airplane assignments." We knew something was wrong. The Air Inspector didn't go around giving check rides. Our instructor referred to his clipboard and continued, "I'll fly the lead airplane, and," looking at the one cadet in our group whom we all knew was having the most problems with his flying, said, "You'll ride in my back seat." He assigned another cadet to fly his left wing and another one to fly on his right wing. He then said, "Wyper, you'll lead the second element. The Air Inspector will ride in your back seat." He assigned the remaining two cadets to fly on my left and right wings. Needless to say, we all realized the gravity of this situation. One goof and we could be instantly washed out. The Air Inspector had much higher authority than the regular check pilots who normally did the washing out.

The Air Inspector, a tall unsmiling major, came over and without any preliminary greeting, said, "We'll take off in two three-ship formations, fly out to the practice area, do some air work, then in six-ship formation do landings and takeoffs at the auxiliary field." That was it — period! No questions, nothing. He just turned and started for the room where we picked up our parachutes. We had never ever done six-ship formation takeoffs and landings before.

I grabbed my parachute and went for my airplane. I found it and did my preflight walk-around inspection while the major climbed into the rear seat. The other five airplanes were also getting underway and we all taxied out to the runup area by the end of the active runway. With tower clearance, my instructor and his two wingmen pulled onto the runway. I moved in behind them with my two wingmen. As wingmen on our instructor we had previously made three-ship formation takeoffs and landings but never six. My instructor and his two wingmen started down the runway. I nodded my head to my fellow cadets on my right and left wing, then eased my throttle forward to full power. They stayed right beside me. Our six airplanes, forming two V's, flew out to the practice area.

The major spoke over the radio for the first time saying, "Now we'll go into string formation and do a few rolls and loops." We all slid into a single line behind our instructor who dived for some additional speed, then pulled up into a very nice barrel roll. We all followed. After several rolls and a couple of loops, the Major came over the radio again, "Now let's see an Immelmann". My instructor obliged and we all followed. Flying the number four spot, it looked good to me. I couldn't see five and six too well, who were behind me, but I knew they were hanging in there. They were both good men. After the Immelmann, the Major spoke again, "Now, back to the six-plane formation and we'll shoot some formation landings and takeoffs." There was even ice in that man's voice. What was with him? Why was he trying to wash us out?

I positioned my three airplanes just as close to the first three as I could. I was flying formation off the first three and my two wingmen were flying formation on me. My instructor, in the lead airplane, made a wide turn onto the final approach. All six airplanes turned as one. As soon as the lead airplane's landing gear started to appear, we all very quickly moved our gear handles to the down and locked position. The auxiliary field was a big dirt field wide enough to adequately handle our six-ship formation landing. Only one man, our instructor in the number one airplane, was landing with visual reference to the ground. The remaining five airplanes were simply flying a tight formation. We never took our eyes off of the airplane on which we were flying formation but we could still see the ground rushing by closer and closer until we all touched down. Even our landing roll out was in formation. We taxied back, turned around and made a six-ship formation takeoff. Our six airplanes climbed out as one, turned to downwind, to base leg, then onto final approach, lowered our landing gear and flaps and landed again. After our second formation takeoff, the Major's voice came over the radio, "Now take the formation back to the main field."

As our tight little formation approached the main field, the Air Inspector addressed our group again, "Now, we'll break off and land invidually." That was fine for everybody else, but he was still in my back seat. I made a good landing, turned off the runway, and was taxiing back to the ramp when he lit into me over the intercom. His cold icy voice came through my earphones, "Mister! You just violated one of the base's flying regulations!" I thought, *My God, what did I do?* I didn't have long to wonder. He came right back, "You pulled up your flaps while you were still rolling! Don't you know that you must taxi off the runway and come to a complete stop and look down at that flap handle before moving it?" I meekly but firmly answered, "Yes Sir!" He said, "There's a very good reason for that regulation. It's to prevent cadets from retracting their landing gear on the runway."

I parked the airplane, shut off the engine, and climbed out. As we walked back to the operations building, he reminded me again about when and how the flaps were to be retracted. I knew that the entire flight had gone extremely well and that I had given him a damn good ride. If the only thing he could find fault with was how I retracted the flaps after landing, I knew we had passed. Some time later, I was told what had prompted that check ride by the Air Inspector. It seemed as the instructors were lounging around in their room when the Air Inspector entered and said that he wanted to see each officer's dog tags. When he found one lieutenant without his he put him on report. The story had it that my instructor expressed in a soft voice, but apparently not soft enough, to one of his friends that he thought that was pretty chickenshit. Overhearing his remark, the Air Inspector ordered the formation check ride. His intent was to wash out some of his students for revenge. Well, we lucked out by giving him an excellent flight demonstration and I was deeply flattered that my instructor must have considered me his best student because he placed me in the most demanding position.

As graduation time grew near, we each had one last ride with our instructors. It was classified as a final check ride, but it was more of a formality because if a cadet was having problems with his flying it would have been discovered long before now and it would have either been corrected or he would have been eliminated.

After takeoff, my instructor spoke to me over the intercom, telling me to do whatever I wanted to do. That kind of threw me. Had he told me to do a six-turn spin, I would have immediately gone into action but I couldn't think of any maneuver that would really be appropriate with him sitting there in the back seat. He knew I could fly the airplane so churning up his breakfast wouldn't prove anything. I just sat there for a while and contemplated the clear blue Texas sky. I thought that I had better do something so I made a couple of gentle clearing turns, then eased the nose down, picked up a little speed and did my favorite maneuver — a slow roll. Having extra long arms was a real asset when it came to doing slow rolls or flying inverted because I could really hold the stick forward which was essential to maintain altitude while flying upside down. It was a good roll with no loss of altitude. Once more I found myself just sitting there looking out over hundreds of miles of Texas when he spoke to me again over the intercom. "Bill," he said, "You'll be graduating in a couple of weeks. Would you like to become an instructor?" This was a real honor. He was giving me the chance to become an instructor. All I had to do was say yes. I knew that all it took was his recommendation and he was asking me if I wanted it. Many of my buddies would have leaped at the chance to become a "stateside" flight instructor — to be a commissioned officer and a pilot and at the same time keep out of the shooting. There was nothing for me to think over. I picked up my mike, pressed the button and said, "No Sir, I want to be a fighter pilot."

The big day finally arrived. The day we had been looking forward to for a long long time. We took off our cadet clothes for the last time and put on our newly purchased officer uniforms and very carefully pinned the gold bars on to the shoulder epaulets. The paper work had already been taken care of in an administrative shuffle. Before we could be sworn in as commissioned officers, we had to be discharged from the army. As aviation cadets, we were enlisted men in the United States Army with army enlisted serial numbers. So right at the height of World War II we received our Honorable Discharges from the Army of the United States. Simultaneously, we were sworn in as Second Lieutenants in the United States Army Air Corps.

We had to buy our own uniforms and even our own gold bars, but the silver wings were presented personally to each new pilot in a fitting ceremony. It was truly a big day. I was now a Second Lieutenant and a rated pilot in the U.S. Army Air Corps. I was nineteen years old.

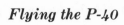

First assignment immediately after graduation was the P-40 training unit based right at Eagle Pass. Our much-deserved first leave since starting in cadets would be after the two-week P-40 course. But our lifestyle was greatly improved. We had moved from the cadet barracks to the bachelor officer quarters. We ate in the officer's mess and at night we went to the officer's club. And now, all of the enlisted men and cadets saluted us.

The P-40 was a single seat fighter so we would be by ourselves on that first flight. There would be no seasoned instructor on board to help us. Therefore, we paid real close attention to what the instructors had to say during our ground school briefings.

The P-40 had already become legendary as the shark-nose fighter of the famous Flying Tigers, General Claire Chennault's American Volunteer Group in China. The first United States aerial victories of World War II were scored by P-40s. On December 7, 1941, as the Japanese air armada descended upon Pearl Harbor, a couple of young Army Air Corps lieutenants of the 15th Pursuit Group leaped into their P-40s and scrambled to the attack. George Welch shot down four of the attacking Japanese aircraft and Harry Brown shot down two.

Throughout the manufacturing life of the P-40, Curtiss engineers and engineers at Allison continued to refine designs and improve performance. As each major change was incorporated, the model letter designation would be changed. We were going to fly the P-40N, the very latest in the long series of P-40s.

The fuselage of the P-40N was over a foot longer than its older sisters. It was also 400 pounds lighter. Its mighty V-12 Allison with 1710 cubic inches was capable of producing 1200 horsepower, twice the horsepower of the Pratt & Whitney engines in the AT-6s.

Our ground school sessions covered every bit of the P-40. They even had cutaway displays of some of the systems and components. One that greatly impressed me was the working model of the fuel system. The pressure carburetor had a plexiglass side on it so you could look right in it as fuel was being pumped in.. The volume of fuel pouring into that carburetor reminded me of water gushing out of a regular garden hose when the valve was wide open.

After all of the systems had been thoroughly explained to us, we were taken to the ramp and shown the real thing. Before we could fly the P-40, we had to pass a written test which was given to us at the conclusion of the ground school and we had to pass a cockpit check, blindfolded. We were allowed to sit in the P-40 as long as necessary to memorize exactly where everything was located. Then we took the test. An instructor would squat down on the wing beside the cockpit while we sat inside with a blindfold over our eyes. He would say, "Point to your fuel gauges." We had three to point to. He would say, "Put your hand on the fuel selector valve." He did the same with the fuel boost pump, oxygen regulator, gun switches, flap handle, gear handle, hydraulic wobble pump, etc. With that out of the way, I was finally ready for that first flight.

If a guy was ever going to get sweaty palms, this would be the time. I swung my parachute on and fastened the chest straps, climbed up into the cockpit, fastened the leg straps and sat down. For this first flight, an instructor was on the wing instead of the crew chief. He helped me with my shoulder harness. I fastened the harness together with my safety belt. Then I connected my oxygen supply and hooked up my microphone and earphones.

Visually working my way around the inside of the cockpit, I was checking the position of every handle, knob, lever, switch and the needles on all of the gauges. The instructors must have figured that we would never be ready on our own because they did a lot of assisting in starting our engines that first time. While I was trying to make sure everything was where it was supposed to be, my instructor was reaching into the cockpit, advancing my throttle handle and moving the mixture control to auto rich. He told me to energize the starter. Before I knew what was happening, the mighty Allison came to life. The loud staccato from its twelve very short exhaust stacks quickly merged into a deafening roar through which no human voice could penetrate. After a thumbs-up gesture, the instructor quickly turned away and leaped off of the wing and scrambled out of the propeller blast. I signalled the crew chief to pull the wheel chocks. I released the parking brakes and started to taxi out to the runway. You really had to "S" while taxiing the P-40. There was no way that you could see past that huge nose when the tail was on the ground.

I pulled up short of the active runway to do my pre-takeoff checks; rudder, elevator and aileron trims all set, mixture auto rich, prop pitch to 2300 RPM, switch mags from both to left, to both, to right, back to both, now set the prop control to 2800 RPM, fuel selector valve to reserve, check fuel pressure, and open the coolant doors. I called the tower and told them I was ready for takeoff. Permission was granted.

I released my toe pressure on the brakes and advanced the throttle enough to pull the four tons out onto the runway. I lined up on the centerline and pushed the throttle all the way forward to its stop. The manifold gauge showed 45 inches of mercury and the tachometer showed 3,000 RPM. As the P-40 roared down the runway I eased the stick forward to bring the tail up. A quick glance at the airspeed told me it was time to ease back on the stick. The P-40 drove up into the sky like a Sherman tank. I touched my toe brakes to stop the wheels from spinning and retracted my landing gear. I pulled the throttle back to 38 inches of manifold pressure and moved the prop back to 2500 RPM.

During that takeoff and climbout, the P-40 gave me the impression of guiding a battleship into the air. That long nose protruding way out in front of me, its heavy weight and its tremendous stability, all contributed to that feeling. It was very different than the AT-6 with which we had become so familiar. I leveled off and pulled the throttle back to 34 inches and the prop to 2200 RPM. I was indicating 240 miles per hour.

The objective of that first flight was to take off, climb up to a reasonably safe altitude, get a general idea of its handling characteristics, try a power-off stall in its landing configuration, then return to the field and land without demolishing the airplane and killing ourselves. The percentage rate of success was amazingly high, mainly because most of us, by now, had become good pilots. One story did make the rounds though concerning a young Chinese pilot who was making his first flight in a P-40 out at Luke Field, near Phoenix, Arizona. He was a member of a special group of Chinese air cadets that had been sent to the United States for flight training. He had managed to get off the ground and had supposedly completed his required air work. His problem was landing.

He came in on final approach too fast and too high. He did have his wheels down, but that wasn't his problem. The tower was hollering at him to "Go around! Go around!" which meant to apply full power, climb back up to pattern altitude, circle back and try again. But the tower's frantic instructions were to no avail. He was determined to land. The speeding P-40's wheels touched the runway but too close to its end for him to possibly stop. With his tail still high in the air, he ran off the end of the runway and blasted through the fence surrounding the field. Both of the main landing gear collapsed as he bounced over the rocks and cactus. In a cloud of dust the badly bent bird finally ground to a stop, its wheels sheared off and all three propeller blades wrapped back around the nose.

When the crash crews arrived at the scene, they couldn't believe their eyes. The young Chinese pilot was still seated in the cockpit casually writing in the form-one. This is the paper work that is normally completed after each flight. It's the aircraft's log book in which squawks are noted, items such as static on the radio, brakes a little weak, etc. After carefully returning the form-one to its usual storage place on the shroud over the instrument panel, the young pilot nonchalantly climbed out of the completely wrecked airplane. The officer, with the crash crew, reached into the cockpit and grabbed the form-one to see what the young Chinese pilot had written. There were five neatly written words, "Airplane O.K., runway too short."

About the only incident that occurred during our two weeks of P-40 training at Eagle Pass was one of the new lieutenants couldn't get his wheels down. When word of his plight came from the tower, the captain in charge of the little P-40 training unit immediately went into action. He more than qualified as a tiger and he looked the part too — he was big and tough. He had just returned from flying P-40s in North Africa.

The two airplanes appeared right on the deck heading toward the field in a very tight formation. The captain literally flew the young lieutenant right into the ground. The lieutenant's P-40 touched down on its belly and the captain pulled up into a standard landing circle, lowered his gear and flaps and landed. Considering it landed on its belly, damage seemed to be minimal and of course, the young lieutenant walked away unscathed.

The P-40's increased performance allowed us to be a little more venturesome. We could fly faster, higher and further than we could in the AT-6s in the same amount of time. Needless to say, we took advantage of that added capability.

The nondescript countryside around Eagle Pass left little in the way of adventure for us in the speedier P-40s. We had become pretty familiar with the surrounding area while flying the AT-6s so with the increased performance I couldn't resist aiming my P-40 in directions where the AT-6 had never ventured.

After takeoff I banked my P-40 to the west toward the afternoon sun and the Rio Grande. As I followed the river north past Del Rio, Texas, I became intrigued with the mountainous terrain off to my left, in Mexico. Knowing full well that I was not supposed to, I banked to my left and descended for a closer look. The jagged cliffs were lavender on top, in the afternoon sunlight, but mysteriously dark and foreboding further down in the gorges. I checked the time, my fuel tanks and my engine instruments. Everything was O.K., so I pressed on down for a close-up look. I had never before seen such a treacherous-looking environment. My 240 miles per hour were magnified as I flashed past the faces of those cliffs. I kept looking around, expecting to possibly see another P-40 exploring the area, but the only signs of life that I saw were a few mountain goats.

With the ten hours of P-40 time in our log books, we packed up and left Eagle Pass. My orders were to report to Headquarters, 72nd Fighter Training Wing, 2nd Air Force, Harding Field, Baton Rouge, Louisiana. The reporting date was thirteen days away so each of us headed in the direction of home. This was our first chance to go home for a visit since we joined up.

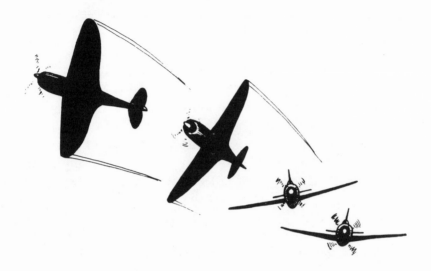

Young second lieutenants with shiny new wings were pouring into Harding Field from all of the single engine advance flying schools in the Central Training Command. We were here to receive our initial briefings as future fighter pilots and to be assigned to a Replacement Training Unit for flight training.

In the early stages of the War, much of the training was done as complete fighter units. Everybody, pilots and all of the ground personnel, trained together in squadrons and groups, then went overseas intact. Now things were different; no more complete units were being formed. Therefore, we would receive our fighter training in a Replacement Training Unit (RTU) and then be assigned to an existing combat unit as a replacement.

Four types of fighter planes were in current use by the various commands. Some bases in the western states were using P-38s, bases in the south and east were still using P-40s and early model P-51s. The 72nd Fighter Wing, to which I had been assigned, were equipped with P-47s at all of their bases except two which were still using P-40s. So it soon became apparent that one of the objectives during this processing period was to convince us that the Republic P-47 Thunderbolt was the greatest fighter plane in the entire world. We were subjected to endless lectures on every aspect of the P-47. The brainwashing strategy became so obvious that it made us subconsciously wonder if, by any chance, was there something wrong with the P-47 that needed this kind of effort to overcome. We just took for granted that it was a good airplane. Otherwise, why would we be using them?

They went to great lengths to give detailed accounts of its rugged durability including the classic story about one pilot who came back from a combat mission and mentioned to his crew chief that his engine seemed to be running a little rough. The crew chief walked around in front of the airplane and spotted the problem. One of its eighteen cylinders was gone. There was a big hole in the cowl where the engine section had taken a direct hit, completely blowing off one of the cylinders.

Aces, just back from the European theater, spoke to us

about the P-47's ability to outfly the Messerschmitt ME-109 and the Focke-Wulf 190. We were convinced that the "Jug" was truly an outstanding fighter plane.

In addition to its function as headquarters for the 72nd Fighter Wing, Harding Field was also one of the training bases. Formations of P-47s were coming and going all day long. We were impressed.

The formation peel-offs prior to landing were really spectacular. Flights of four P-47s would come roaring in toward the runway on their initial approach. When they reached the threshold-end of the runway, the leader would pull up into a tight climbing turn. At about one-second intervals, the number two man would pull up, then number three and four. As soon as they started the pull ups they would come back on their throttles. The purpose of the tight climbing turns was to kill off excess speed so their landing gear could be lowered and to get spacing between each airplane before landing. These pitch-out maneuvers were made even more spectacular by the high Louisiana summer humidity. As each P-47 would pull up, white streamers of condensed water vapor would trail off behind both wingtips forming big white arcs in the sky. This was a tough couple of weeks for us, watching those P-47s every day while we sat on the ground through one lecture after another.

Processing was finally completed and we received our orders. I was assigned to a place that I had never even heard of ... Fort Sumner, New Mexico ... to fly P-40s. After all of that brainwashing, I was kind of looking forward to flying the big P-47s.

Eagle Pass sounded like a place where future fighter pilots should be flying but Fort Sumner, New Mexico sounded like the U.S. Cavalry and Indians.

During the train ride from Louisiana to New Mexico, we discovered that in addition to all of us being second lieutenants heading for fighter pilot training, we had one more thing in common. We were all bachelors. Graduation from flying school and weddings went hand in hand for a number of our buddies, but none of them were on this train. When the assignments were announced, back at Baton Rouge, they told us that the very small community of Fort Sumner, New Mexico, had no housing accommodations for dependents. Knowing that the newly married officers would bring their wives anyway, they must have gone through our files and picked this all-bachelor group for Fort Sumner. One bunch was assigned to train right there at Harding Field in Baton Rouge. Another group was sent to the resort town of Colorado Springs, and here we were being shipped out to a desolate spot in New Mexico. We looked forward to flying and we also looked forward to the possibility of a little extracurricular social life, but where we were going, the prospects of the latter seemed dubious.

Small as it was, the air base complex of hangars, barracks, messhall and hospital, was larger than the "town" of Fort Sumner. If you were driving through New Mexico and saw the sign pointing to Billy the Kid's grave, that was Fort Sumner.

The airfield had just recently been taken over by the 72nd Fighter Training Wing. It had been a glider pilot training facility. I guess the army figured they had enough glider pilots

to handle their planned invasions. Now, neat rows of P-40s
lined the two large ramps which formed an L on two sides of
the complex of buildings. All of the P-40s on the south ramp
sported red spinners and all of the P-40s on the east ramp had
yellow noses. I was assigned to the training squadron on the
east ramp which had the yellow noses.

They started us out on formation flying, but instead of the
three-ship V formations like we flew in advance, we now flew
in four-plane fighter formations. A formation of two fighters
was called an element. A formation of two elements was called
a flight and a formation of four flights made up a squadron,
which was sixteen airplanes. The thing that impressed me
during those first formation flights was how rock-steady the
P-40s appeared compared to the AT-6s which, being much
lighter, had a tendency to bounce around.

From a human engineering point of view, the cockpit of the
P-40 left a few things to be desired. The landing gear system
was the best, or rather the worst example. We would come in
on our initial approach usually in flights of four. Before
reaching the field we would go into an echelon right
formation. The leader would be on the left and the other three
aircraft would be on his right. We would slow down to about
200 to 220 miles per hour. While approaching the field in this
tight echelon formation, we would reach down with our left
hand and move the landing gear handle/valve mechanism
from its locked position to the down position. All this did was
open up the main valve. Nothing really happened to move the
gear except you could always tell when the pilot next to you
had moved his handle to the down position because his tail
wheel would drop down and partially open the tail wheel
doors. When each four-plane formation reached the boundary
of the field, the number one airplane would pull up into a steep
climbing turn with the others following at about one second
intervals, just as the P-47s did at Harding Field. As soon as we

started the tight climbing turn, we'd press a little trigger on the control stick with the little finger of our right hand. (Our left hand would be pulling the throttle back.) The little trigger on the control stick actuated an electric motor which pumped hydraulic pressure into the system to force down the landing gear. As the main gear rotated and moved down out of the wings, small pegs moved up out of the topside of the wings as visual indicators for the pilot. The top of each peg was red, the middle was yellow and the bottom was green. When you saw the green of both left and right pegs you could assume that your two main wheels were in their down positions. Now you quickly changed hands, holding the control stick with your left hand while you furiously pumped the hydraulic hand pump on the right side of the cockpit. You'd rapidly work it back and forth until it became very stiff indicating that the hydraulic lines in the landing gear system had full pressure. Then you'd quickly change hands again, now holding the control stick with your right hand, you would use your left hand to reach down and return the gear handle/valve back up to its locked position. All the time you're doing this you're getting spacing off the P-40 ahead and putting down flaps in preparation to land. As complicated as it sounds, we could do it very fast without really giving it too much thought.

Another frailty of the P-40 was its electric prop. On rare occasions, if the aircraft's electrical system got too low, the propeller would automatically go into high pitch. The hand book said that you could manually override this by holding the three-way toggle switch, on the instrument panel, in the low pitch position but accidents did happen.

I had just landed one morning when I heard the tower hollering, "Go around! Go around!" I knew he was talking to the next landing airplane which had to be the guy right behind me. More frantic commands came from the tower, "Give it the throttle! Give it the throttle!" I looked up into my wide rearview mirror, which was inside the top of my windshield, and there he was. He was flying but just barely as he went over top of me. His engine was wide open but his propeller wasn't doing its job. I could see him settling down in front of me. His wheels were already retracting which didn't matter anyway because there was no runway left. He went into the sagebrush in a big cloud of dust. The airplane was heavily damaged but he lucked out and walked away.

We were here to qualify as fighter pilots. Our next assignment would be combat. Every bit of our training was now directed toward achievement of that goal — to make us expert fighter pilots. To become a successful fighter pilot, to possess the skills to engage and kill the enemy and not get ourselves killed, we had to become the complete master of our aircraft. The term for this type of flying is Maximum Performance.

In fighter pilot terminology, maximum performance means flying your airplane to its absolute limits in all maneuvers. We were to learn just how tight you could make a turn without hitting a high-speed stall, how steep you could climb without falling out of the sky, how fast you could dive without tearing it apart and how many Gs you could pull before completely passing out. We were to find out all of these things for ourselves because our P-40s were single seaters. Nobody would be riding with us to show us how.

Sometimes, during most every formation flight, the leader would signal for us to get into string formation. His wingman would slide underneath and just a little behind. The leader of the second element would move in behind the number two man, then his wingman would drop in behind him and so on until all of the airplanes were in a single file "follow the leader" formation. Then the fun would start. In the Army Air Corps it was called a rat race. The Navy called theirs a "tail chase". The leader would do whatever he felt like and the rest of us would follow. The degree of challenge, to your piloting skills, depended upon your position in that line of airplanes. If you were up toward the head end, number two, three or four, it wasn't too tough, but if you were toward the end, say six, seven or eight, you were getting into the realm of maximum performance flying. It could be compared to the old game of crack-the-whip where the kid on the end really got whipped around.

The leader would start out by diving for speed. In order to keep the last man from stalling out, the leader would have to carry more speed through the maneuvers than if he were doing them by himself. He might split-S, do a half roll to the inverted position, then pull back on the stick, sending his airplane down through a half loop. The string of airplanes would follow. The leader then might do a couple of slow rolls and maybe a barrel roll and then pull up into an Immelmann or a couple of loops. Because of varying skill levels among the young second lieutenants, these rat races sometimes got pretty hairy. The single-file formation of airplanes, going through the various aerobatic maneuvers, could be compared to a chain. One weak link could break the chain. If any pilot dropped back or lost his position, all of the airplanes behind him would be affected. One day, about six of us were rat racing around in the sunny New Mexico sky and I was the pilot who broke the chain.

I was flying in the very best spot, number two, right behind the leader. Four other P-40s were behind me. After the usual loops, rolls and Immelmanns, our leader cranked it around into a tight climbing turn. Priding myself on being a real hot pilot, I would never let any space develop between my airplane and the one I was following. I'd stay glued right to his tail. The top of my propeller would be just inches below his tail wheel doors, but this time he turned right into the sun. After the blinding flash of direct sun, I regained sight of the P-40 ahead.

He was still turning, but contrary to my usual style of flying, the space between our two airplanes was considerable. I pulled back hard on the stick to close the gap. He was in a tight vertical bank but I managed to get back into position. We were really in a maximum performance Lufbery circle. We were pulling heavy G-loads and at the same time the stick forces were getting very light which meant I was on the verge of a high speed stall. About that time I heard our leader's voice over the radio saying, "Wyper, what the hell are you doing?" I suddenly realized what had happened. I eased the stick forward and moved out of the extremely tight Lufbery. The four P-40s followed me as I rejoined with our leader who had been sitting up-sun watching us do probably the wildest little tail chase he had ever seen. After that momentary blinding by the sun, the airplane that I spotted and joined up on, was not the leader, but tail-end charlie. So in effect we were really chasing our own tail.

On a couple of occasions we flew practice intercept missions against formations of B-17s. I guess both sides were supposed to benefit from the exercise, but one thing for sure, it was lots of fun for us.

We arrived at the rendezvous point with an altitude advantage so we could initiate the simulated attack with vertical dives down through their formation. Two by two we rolled over and headed straight down toward the bombers. As we flashed by I caught a glimpse of their many guns trying to track us. But being very close and fast, I think we would have won had it been a real contest. After passing through the formation, their bottom turret gunners would get the last chance at us but our speed would certainly have been to our advantage. Far below the bombers, we'd pull out and start climbing back up for another pass.

Pulling out of those dives really unrolled our socks. On some of the pullouts, even my oxygen mask was forced down off of my face. Then as the G-forces decreased, the straps holding it to my helmet would pull the mask back up but it would always catch against the bottom of my nose. Using the hose as a handle, I'd lift the mask up over my nose and let it back into position over my nose and mouth.

At the bottom of those dives, the needle on my airspeed indicator would be right on the 480 miles per hour red line and that combination of high speed and high G-loads was hard on both plane and pilot. We'd be squashed down in our seats by as much as seven or eight times the force of normal gravity. I weighed about 175 pounds, but during some of those pullouts, I'd weigh almost three-fourths of a ton and that made for heavy arms and legs. We were building up pretty good tolerances against the G-forces, but the human body could withstand just so much. Our vision was the first thing affected as the G-forces increased. We would get what they called tunnel vision. Gray would start to move in from the outer edges of our field of vision just as though we were looking through a gray pipe. If we kept hauling back on the stick, increasing the G-forces, the gray would keep moving in toward the center of our field of vision until everything became a solid gray. Sight was gone. That was called "graying out". If you continued to haul back on the stick, increasing the G-forces, the field of gray changed to black. At that point your brain didn't have enough blood to keep you conscious. The instant you blacked out, the muscle power that you were applying to hold the stick back would be involuntarily released. That reduced the G-forces and consciousness would quickly return. We became well acquainted with these side effects and soon learned how to coordinate the amount of Gs with the degree of incapacitation that we were willing to endure in any particular situation. Generally speaking, the airplanes were stronger than we were, but there were exceptions.

One of the pilots in our attacking force apparently overdid it because as he was pulling out, he pulled off one of his ailerons. It was dangling from one hinge point. The pilots behind him seemed more concerned about it than he was. Very excited radio voices apprised him that his left aileron had ripped out. His cool acknowledgement surprised all of us. In his very familiar southern drawl, he said, "Yeah, . . . I see it. I'll stop up here a ways and get out and fix it." He had no problem getting back to Fort Sumner and landing. But his luck was to later run out over Japan in a P-51. He was killed.

One thing nice about Fort Sumner was that we were surrounded by hundreds of miles of barren land over which we could practice the art of low altitude flying and I mean low altitude like four or five feet above the ground. The instructors didn't want us to fly that low so they flew along behind continually hollering at us to pull up. On these low altitude training missions we'd usually fly out from the field in the standard four-ship fighter formation. Then the instructor would have his wingman and the other two airplanes fan out into a very loose line abreast formation so that each pilot could keep an eye on the ground. The instructor would fly along behind us at a slightly higher altitude and constantly holler at us to pull up.

One early morning, the area was covered by a thin layer of ground fog which was so thin and so close to the ground that tops of trees, farm houses and windmills could be seen sticking through the solid white ground cover. From above, this ground fog looked like a regular layer of stratus clouds that could have been thousands of feet above the ground, if it weren't for the occasional tree or windmill poking through into the bright sunlight. So instead of flying along over the ground, this time we were buzzing along on top of the clouds with the ever-present instructor bringing up the rear, hollering to pull up. The order went unheeded by one of the young second lieutenants whose prop was cutting a swath in the cloud tops. As he zipped dangerously close to a protruding windmill, it happened.

He knew he was in trouble — that he had hit something. His speeding P-40 had been severely jolted. He eased back on the stick to gain some altitude and a chance to assess the damage. The instructor moved in beside him for a closer look. A heavy steel cable was wrapped around his right wing and trailing clear back past his tail. A piece of flat steel about two feet long was flapping on one of the cable ends. It was hitting his horizontal stabilizer. After he nursed it back to Fort Sumner and landed, we all got a close-up look at the results of that incredible accident.

As he flew past that windmill, his right wing tip missed the main section of the vertical structure but struck a steel cable which served as a guy wire. Fortunately for him, the force of his speeding P-40 snapped the cable loose at both ends. If one end had held, the accident would have been catastrophic. The P-40's rugged construction had saved his life. That cable knifed through his wing's leading edge all the way to the front spar.

Most of our training flights combined several activities. In addition to the customary formation takeoffs and general air work, there would be special objectives to accomplish. These sometimes included on-the-deck passes across our strafing range.

About thirty miles southeast of our base, some dummy wood and cloth airplanes were scattered along several miles of rocks and sagebrush. Sometimes we'd just buzz the place. Other times we used our guns. Sometimes two of our guns would have ammo, one in each wing, and on at least one flight all six were loaded so we could feel what it was like to fire six fifty-calibers at one time. It was amazing how they slowed down the airplane.

As we neared the range, we'd turn on our gun sights. An

amber ring and pipper was projected on a canted glass which was mounted above the instrument panel, in our direct line of sight. A rheostat controlled its brightness. If it was pretty dark outside, you'd turn it way down. In bright sunlight it would be turned full up.

We would usually, hit the range in flights of four. We'd spread out in a wide line-abreast formation and head for the deck. I could see the other airplanes kicking up dust on both sides of me, but we were on our own as far as when we chose to fire. We could bob up and down and fire whenever we wanted to. There were enough of those dummy wood and cloth targets for everybody.

Sometimes as targets would appear up ahead, we'd pull up a little so we could make a longer descending firing pass. Even with the cooling effect of the wind, created by the airplane's flying speed, the gun barrels could be easily overheated and destroyed if the firing bursts were longer than just a couple of seconds. If you could keep the target in your sights longer, the proper technique was to fire a short burst, let up on the trigger for a second or two, then fire another short burst. When the barrels overheated, the bore apparently enlarged because the bullets, at least the tracers — the ones you could see — came out like orange baseballs tumbling and going in all directions. Whenever the strafing airplanes got strung out, the worst place to be was up front. More than once I'd find myself flying formation with somebody else's bullets that had bounced off of the ground.

It was amazing how the recoil from those six 50-calibers slowed down the airplane. Even a short burst was like chopping the throttle. If you fired a long burst in a slow nose-high attitude, their combined recoil could actually cause the airplane to stall.

In small groups, we were sent down to Galveston, Texas, for two weeks of extensive air-to-air gunnery training. All gunnery missions were flown out over the Gulf of Mexico. When schedules permitted, extracurricular missions were staged forty miles to the northwest in the fine city of Houston, a pleasant respite for the young bachelors from Fort Sumner.

We always flew out in formation and set up a pattern on the airplane towing the target just like we did in advance flying school, but unlike advance, when our guns were empty, we'd frequently leave and individually fly back to our base at Galveston. It was on these return flights that I reached my highest speeds in the P-40. Some of our gunnery missions were flown at 20,000 feet so when we were done, we'd just roll over and head for Galveston. Because the P-40s were built like tanks, the thought never occurred to me that anything could ever give way, and it didn't either, although it was impossible to hold the ball in the center, even by standing on the left rudder. When the airspeed reached its upper limits it was impossible to keep it in trim. It just wasn't made to go 500 miles per hour.

Our time at Galveston was divided between three major activities, the daily missions out over the Gulf, shooting at those banner targets, the few night missions to Houston, and taking our turn in the "Gunair Instructor".

The "Gunair Instructor" could be compared to some sophisticated device that you might expect to find in an amusement arcade. It was housed in a Quonset-hut-like structure inside one of the big hangars. After you entered, a roll down door was closed to keep out any light. An open type cockpit was bolted to a concrete pedestal about a couple of feet above the hangar floor. Dummy wings protruded about two feet on each side of the cockpit. I was instructed to get into the cockpit. I climbed up onto the stubby wing and into the cockpit just as I would on a real airplane. The instructor pointed out the obvious controls including the rheostat which controlled the intensity of the gunsight. The gun trigger was in its usual place on the control stick. The instructor took his position at another set of controls down in front of my cockpit. Then the action began.

The room lights went black and the wall in front of us lit up with clouds and a white silhouette of an airplane. That was the enemy. My job was to shoot it down. The white airplane on the screen rolled into a bank and sped away. I advanced my throttle to its stop and took up the chase. As I pushed my stick to the side to go into the bank, the horizon on the screen swung to a vertical position. The sensation was uncannily realistic. The white airplane was still in a 90-degree bank but it was getting larger. I was gaining on him. The accurate coordination of the visual display combined with the audible roar of my engine, seemed so real that I would have sworn that I was actually experiencing G-forces as I pulled back harder on the stick trying to put the pipper of my gunsight far enough ahead of him to score hits. I squeezed the trigger, my guns banged away and just like in the penny arcades, every time I scored a hit, the white airplane on the screen flashed red.

But how long can you play in a penny arcade? As realistic as the Gunair Instructor seemed, it was no match for the way we spent the other half of our days, miles above the blue water of the Gulf, firing real bullets into targets traveling 200 miles an hour. Showing up for our scheduled stint in the Gunair Instructor interfered with our excursions up to Houston, but we soon found a solution.

In one corner of the same large hangar that housed the Gunair Instructor, graduate bombardiers rode around on top of weird elevated devices that crept along while they aimed their bomb sights at maps painted on the floor. They had heard about the fun the fighter pilots were having in that Quonset hut over on the other side of the hangar so they asked us if there was any chance they could try it. We seized upon the opportunity. We told them they could most certainly have a ride in it if they signed the log sheet for us. We gave them our names and took off for Houston and another night on the town.

We were supposed to complete a specified number of air-to-air gunnery missions during our two weeks at Galveston, but the weather was not cooperating. We had reported to flight operations on schedule that morning but it was still pouring rain outside with about a four hundred foot ceiling. The commanding officer of the fighter gunnery squadron, a major, came into the room and announced that he would take up one flight. He got on the phone and told whoever pulled our targets to take one up and wait for us "on top" out over the Gulf. He then asked who would like to go. Several of us held up our hands. I was picked to fly his wing. Because this was not going to be one of our easy sunny flights, he picked one of the instructors, a captain, to lead the second element. Another second lieutenant trainee was picked to fly his wing. The captain suggested that if he took the two-seater another trainee could go along as an observer. The C.O. agreed. There was a modified P-40 at Galveston which had a second seat installed behind the pilot, in the space normally occupied by our fuselage gas tank. He asked who would like to go along for the ride. The "Judge" volunteered. Each of us had acquired a personalized nickname during our early flying at Fort Sumner. These nicknames provided a means of identifying ourselves to each other over the radio but not to any authorities who might be listening on that same frequency. Most of our nicknames, like Bat, Snake and Doc, had no particular significance, but in the Judge's case it did. He had been a prelaw student and we all felt that he would eventually become a lawyer and maybe even a judge. He was also a big man, at least six-two. A much shorter man would surely have been more comfortable in the cramped space behind the pilot in that two-seater.

The major explained that we would have to make a four-ship formation takeoff and all stay tucked close together so we could see each other as he would be flying by instruments to get us up through the clouds. We put on our Mae Wests (inflatable life preservers), picked up our parachutes and headed out into the rain to find our airplanes.

A steady drizzle was falling from the solid overcast as the four P-40s moved out onto the runway. The major nodded his head and advanced his throttle. My left wing was between his right wing and tail. We sped down the runway, lifted off, and just as our wheels were folding into our wings, we were engulfed by the clouds. My job was easy. I simply flew formation on him while he flew by his instruments.

The P-47 that was pulling our target had taken off earlier so he was already on top. The major asked him, on the radio, how high the tops were. The reply was "about six thousand." It seemed like an eternity as I sat there with my eyes riveted on him while his eyes were riveted on his gauges.

When climbing up through overcasts, most pilots have the tendency to inch the stick back a little more each time the clouds seem to get a little lighter and they think they are about to break out on top. The major was no exception. I could sense our climb steepening each time the cloud seemed to get a little lighter.

We finally broke out into the sparkling sunshine, into the blue sky above the sea of white, but just as we did, a call came over our earphones. The excited voice of the P-47 pilot, who was pulling our target, said that he just saw one of our P-40s roll over and fall back into the clouds. The major leaned over for a backward look. I took a quick glance back too and sure enough, there was only one P-40 back there where there were supposed to be two. The major called back to the captain, thinking that it had to be the second lieutenant wingman who was missing but that was not the case. The second lieutenant was still with us. The captain and the Judge were missing. The three of us circled around while the major kept calling to the captain. An answer finally came. The captain said that he was on his way back up to rejoin us. So we continued to circle over the area where he had disappeared but we were more than a thousand feet above the cloud tops, just in case he might pop up right underneath us.

Eventually, the lone P-40 was spotted across the sea of white clouds, making his way toward us. Once more a four-plane formation, we headed for the P-47 with the target and completed a routine gunnery mission. Our return back to base was uneventful. We made a formation letdown through the clouds, found the field and landed. Their story was unfolded back in the operations shack. Still carrying our parachutes, we gathered around to listen.

Because of its two-seat modification and an exceptionally large man in that back seat, their center of gravity was undoubtedly further aft than on our stock P-40s. That could very easily give them a slightly higher stalling speed. Each time those clouds seemed a little lighter, the major had steepened his climb. The low pressure on my own control stick indicated that a stall was not far away but it was obviously closer for the two-seater because they fell out of the formation. Just as we broke out on top, they stalled, rolled over and headed straight down into the clouds.

A P-40 with its nose down is normally in very good shape, but they still had many degrees of nose-high elevator trim rolled in from that long formation climb up through the clouds. Speed built up quickly, then because of all that nose-high trim, the nose came up and up. They did a complete loop in the clouds before the captain was able to get the elevator trim control turned back to normal. From then on it was simply back to the basics of instrument flying, needle centered, by the stick's side-to-side movement, ball centered by the rudders, and airspeed regulated by the stick's forward and aft movements. He finally got everything under control and they climbed back up to join us.

Our fighter training was rapidly drawing to a close and we at least thought we were ready to take on any enemy. If we weren't hot pilots by now, we were in big trouble because in a matter of weeks we expected to be flying against the Axis powers with both sides using real bullets. By this time we felt very comfortable in our P-40s. We pretty much knew just what it could do and what it couldn't do. We were constantly testing it and ourselves.

One day while out by myself boring holes in the sky, I wondered exactly what the P-40 would do when it stalled out of an absolutely vertical attitude. While pondering that thought, I found myself pulling the nose straight up to find out. I watched the needle on the airspeed indicator slowly unwind until it reached zero. At zero airspeed in this attitude I knew that a four-ton airplane can't just sit there in the sky. I had to be falling tail first, but the airspeed indicator would have no way of telling me how fast. I was careful not to move any of the controls because I knew that would change things very abruptly. The P-40's big nose slowly started moving to the right of its vertical position, literally rotating until the nose was finally pointing straight down. That was neat. I tried to visualize how that would have looked from another vantage point. About that time I spotted another P-40 heading toward me. I immediately turned into him. Fighter pilots always "attack" each other. It becomes instinct. The reason for our being, for our training, is to be the aggressor. The fighter pilot and his purpose is probably best described as the one guy who gets up every morning and goes out looking for a fight.

We churned around in the sky for a while, then I headed for the deck with him right behind me. The wide-angle rear view mirrors just inside the top of our windshields gave us a fair rearward view.

A favorite pastime was buzzing everything in sight, within reason of course. We didn't want to get into trouble so most of us did our buzzing in the wide open spaces with an occasional pass at cattle, cowboys, sheep, sheepherders and a few Indians. I'm positive that the cowboys took potshots at us for scattering their cattle, but they always missed.

I was skimming along right on the deck. The P-40 behind me couldn't get any lower so to keep out of my prop wash, he was flying a few feet higher which put him in good view in my rearview mirror.

My left fist clinched the throttle which was all the way forward to maximize the sensation of speed, to blur the reddish ground, rocks and sagebrush. On a momentary impulse I thought, why not do it right now. After all you are a qualified fighter pilot. I pulled the stick back a little and pushed it all the way to the left and at the same time working rudders, first full right rudder then neutral, stick full forward, "POP," then full left rudder, stick back and rudders to neutral. I had done it! I had proven to myself that I could do it, that I had to guts to do it. I had done a slow roll right on the deck. And, by God, that P-40 behind me had done one too! Just as I rolled out, I caught a glimpse of him in my rearview mirror, completing his roll. But what was that pop that I heard just as I rolled onto my back?

Then it dawned on me. I was so tense as I rolled over, my left hand tightened on the throttle knob which contains the mike button. I had squeezed the mike button, making that pop. I pulled up a little and wiggled my wings, signaling the man behind me to come up alongside. He did. He was one of my best friends. We were both grinning from ear to ear. We now considered ourselves real tigers.

One of the other young tigers did a dumb thing one

morning when he had a solo airplane scheduled for that afternoon. He went to the Western Union office on the base and sent a telegram to a friend in his hometown of Lubbock, Texas, which was about 140 miles from Fort Sumner. Its contents were revealed to the military authorities on the field. His message said, "Be at the highway overpass at 2:00 P.M. and watch me fly under it."

Time on airstrips in combat zones was traditionally precious. The objective for departing formations was to get everybody into the air as quickly as possible and the reverse applied to landing formations. For this reason, we were taught and expected to make tight patterns. Echelons of P-40s would come speeding in toward the runway, then fan up into a beautiful pattern of follow-the-leader, getting spacing, lowering wheels and flaps and landing, as close as possible to the man ahead. You couldn't overrun the guy ahead so when landing in formation your pattern could only be as tight as the airplane you were following. But, when you were by yourself, you had no excuse for making a sloppy pattern. Your performance was measured in seconds. The time they counted was the time between when you pitched up and out of your initial approach and the instant your wheels touched the runway. Thirty seconds was considered O.K. When you got down into the twenties you were really achieving maximum performance. It took almost that long to get the landing gear down and locked. Anything less than about twenty-two seconds, you were dead. My roommate proved that. He prided himself on his super-tight patterns, but one day he pulled it a little too tight. He stalled and crashed. His mistake was fatal.

We had to be in our squadron ready room on the flight line by 7:30 each morning. We always made it on time but usually without breakfast. First flights got off the ground about 8 A.M. The pilots not in those first flights would have an opportunity to grab a cup of coffee and a donut. That was our standard breakfast. The first flights would be flown on empty stomachs. Those pilots would have to wait for their coffee and donuts. This particular morning, I was scheduled in the first flight. It would be a low-level formation cross-country.

The purpose of this flight would be to simulate conditions encountered when penetrating enemy territory. Our formation would fly as close to the ground as possible, the way it was actually done in combat to avoid radar detection.

A captain would be leading the formation totaling six P-40s. The position assignments were made. One lieutenant was assigned to fly his wing. I was assigned the number three spot which would be the element leader. A good friend of mine was assigned to fly my wing. Another lieutenant was assigned to the number five spot and another lieutenant was assigned to fly his wing. The captain briefed us, explaining that we would take off in the standard two-plane formations, join up and then remain on the deck for the entire triangular cross-country. He would do the navigation. The airplane assignments were made. We wrote down the number of our assigned airplane.

When formation flights were scheduled, one additional airplane was usually listed as the spare. We would always write down its number, so if for any reason our assigned airplane could not be used, we would take the spare. We picked up our parachutes and headed for the ramp to find our airplanes.

When I arrived at my assigned airplane, I was informed by the crew chief that it was down because he was changing the battery. That meant I had to hurry and find the spare. The other pilots were getting into their airplanes.

When I finally located it, I couldn't believe what I saw, but the numbers matched. The spare aircraft was brand new. Every P-40 at Fort Sumner was painted olive drab but not this one. It was sparkling aluminum and it was parked right at the apex of the two L-shaped ramps, right in front of the headquarters building. But the numbers matched and time was running out. The other pilots had already started their engines.

The crew chief helped me with my straps and stuff. I started the engine and he pulled the chocks.

I caught up with my group as they were taxiing out onto the runway. I got into position behind the first two airplanes. My wingman pulled up beside me and off we went down the runway, two by two, by two. Once clear of the field our formation descended to sagebrush height and headed north toward our first checkpoint.

Fighter aircraft have a very practical way of compensating for speed differential in turns. For example, two fighters, an element leader and his wingman, are flying on a straight course: the wingman is on his leader's left and slightly behind. If the leader makes a turn to the right, his wingman simply slides underneath him and takes up position on his right wing. This procedure of cutting to the inside of turns eliminates the necessity of big changes in power settings. On the other hand, whenever an element leader turns into his wingman, the wingman simply drops down and slides to the outside of the turn. These smooth and easy changes became second nature.

About eighty miles north of the field, we made our first turn. The captain and his wingman made a turn to their left. My wingman was on my left. We were right on the deck. A level turn would have been impossible because he would have no room to slide under me to go to the outside of the turn. So I did the correct maneuver for such a turn on the deck into a wingman. I first pulled up to give him plenty of room to slide under me on his way to the outside of the turn. He was flying very close to me. As I banked into the turn, I glanced at him. His eyes were naturally glued onto me. He slid underneath me. I continued the turn. Then it happened!

My airplane was racked by the violent impact and the sickening sound of crunching metal. My head whirled around and there was one of his olive drab wings folded over my shiny aluminum right wing. Behind my right trailing edge I saw his airplane, minus a wing, as it flipped into the ground and exploded. The big chunk of olive drab metal rolled off under my wing. My engine had stopped. I pulled the throttle back and tried easing it on but nothing happened. I had to act fast. I yanked the handle to jettison my canopy. It hit my right shoulder as it came off. I would liked to have pulled up and bailed out but that was impossible because I was right on the deck with no engine and my airplane was rapidly decelerating. As soon as the canopy came off, the rushing air whipped my oxygen mask into my face. It had been hanging by its straps on one side of my helmet because at this low altitude it wasn't needed. I had to see what I was doing so I reached up and jerked my helmet off, in order to get rid of that mask that was whipping around in my face. I looked at the tops of my wings. They looked O.K. I looked at my airspeed indicator. Its needle was at 170 miles per hour. Not wanting to hit the ground any faster than necessary, I put down my flaps. That was a mistake. My airplane rolled over to the left into a nose-down vertical bank straight for the ground less than a hundred feet away. I was holding full opposite stick and top rudder but it had no effect. I thought, well now I'll know what it's like to be in an exploding airplane. I had just seen my buddy go and here I was heading for the same fate.

I hit the ground with the nose down and the wings still vertical. There was a seemingly unending succession of violent impacts, metal wrenching and tearing, dirt, oil, fuel, and plexiglass flying. Each impact seemed more violent than the preceding one. But finally it came to a stop. The cockpit section stopped in an upright position. I stepped out onto the ground. I realized that I wasn't breathing so I sat down on my parachute, which was still fastened to my rump, and tried to get some air into my lungs. Blood was pouring down over my eyes, causing me to think that maybe my head was busted. I reached up with both hands to test it as you would a melon or a head of lettuce. It didn't give so I figured the blood must be coming from superficial cuts. I looked at my wrist to see what time it was, and discovered that my watch was gone. There was a cut on my wrist where something had also cut my watchband. I took off my parachute and stood up. The remaining four P-40s were circling low overhead. I waved to them to signal that I was O.K.

Pretty soon a single P-40 made a low pass and just when he got overhead, he dropped a yellow streamer which came floating down and landed not far from where I was. These weighted envelopes, which had about a three-foot yellow ribbon, were carried in our cockpits for this very purpose. I opened the envelope and took out the message which the captain had written on a page out of his airplane's form-one. The note said, "There is a highway, about four miles north of here, in the direction that I am flying when I drop this." The captain was very thoughtful to mention the direction, because I thought he was flying due south. There was a heavy overcast blocking out the sun and any possibility of shadows and that violent cartwheeling, as my airplane broke up, had me completely turned around.

That brand new airplane was totally destroyed. The fuselage was broken into three sections and both wings were torn off. As I looked at that mass of scattered wreckage, I couldn't help but think to myself, how the base commander was going to feel when he learns what has happened to his brand new personal airplane.

When I looked into the cockpit for my watch, it was easy to see what had knocked the wind out of me. The seat had been torn loose and was resting on the rudder pedal tracks almost up against the instrument panel. Its back section, where it was attached to the armor plate, was ripped clear out.

The single thing that saved my life was the fact that I had long arms. We always took off with our shoulder straps locked. Immediately after takeoff, most pilots with normal length arms would have to release the locking mechanism of their harness so they could reach the various knobs and handles in the cockpit. But because of my extra long arms, I could reach everything with my harness still locked and on that particular flight I simply had not bothered to unlock it. The shoulder harness mechanism was tied to the armor plate so even after my seat broke loose, the locked shoulder harness held my head back to at least keep my face from being smashed in by the gun sight. I found my wristwatch with its busted strap and started out on my walk to that highway four miles north.

We had always been told to fly in our G.I. hightop shoes. Well, here I was tramping across the wilds of New Mexico in my shiny new Florsheims. I knew then why they told us to wear our G.I. hightops.

After a while my right knee started to hurt. I looked down and noticed that the maps, in the right knee pocket of my flying suit, were torn. I could see that my flying suit was also torn. I pulled up that pantleg and saw that my winter dress slacks, which I was wearing underneath my flying suit, were torn in the same place. I reluctantly pulled up that pantleg and there just below my knee was a large puncture type of hole in my leg, about an inch in diameter and about an inch deep. I immediately rolled back down both pantlegs and resumed walking. Then I encountered something I hadn't expected, a very large herd of cattle.

I was a city boy and to me, their tremendous numbers plus the massive front that they presented, caused me to worry. I knew I couldn't outrun them and there were no trees to climb. They started to move toward me. There weren't even any good rocks to throw at them. I threw some twigs and hollered. I started to walk again. They started to move toward me again. We went through that entire sequence several times before their curiosity waned. I was later told by some of the natives that I did in fact have reason for concern because those range cattle never see a man on foot. All they see are cowboys on horses and just out of curiosity, a moving herd of that size could trample a man on foot.

I got to the road and before long a tanker truck and trailer came boiling down the road. He was really hauling so it took him a while to get stopped. I'm sure the last thing he expected to see on that desolate road in the middle of New Mexico was a lone man in a flying suit, covered with blood. He jumped out and came running back toward me. I explained that I had been in an airplane accident and asked if he would take me in the direction that he was traveling until I could find a place to make a phone call. He naturally obliged. I must have really been a sight.

The first thing we came upon was one of those last-chance type of gas stations that you find out in the middle of nowhere. He stopped and let me out. I thanked him.

I pulled out my torn maps to find out just where I was so I could tell them, once I got on the phone. I noticed that about five miles west of where I was, the map showed a TWA auxiliary field. That meant a big smooth dirt field that an airplane could land on in an emergency. That gave me an idea.

I placed a long distance collect call to the director of flight operations, Fort Sumner Army Air Base. Major Jones answered the phone. I told him where I was and offered the suggestion. I mentioned that my map showed a TWA auxiliary field about five miles west of where I was. I suggested the possibility that if someone would fly one of the base's two AT-6s out to that auxiliary field, I could get a lift back to base. There were two AT-6s at Fort Sumner which were used as instrument trainers. Major Jones said that he would fly one of them out there to pick me up. I said that I wasn't sure how long it would take me to get there. He said that didn't matter, that if he got there first, he would wait for me. That seemed like a fine solution because it was now afternoon and I had already experienced one hell of a morning and without any coffee and donuts.

As I walked out of that "last-chance" service station, the caravan of emergency vehicles from Fort Sumner came thundering down the road. They saw me and turned into the service station. They told me to get into the ambulance. I told the flight surgeon, a major who was in the ambulance, that I had to go to that auxiliary field, in the opposite direction than they were going, to meet Major Jones who was flying out there to pick me up. The flight surgeon said, "Fuck Major Jones! You're going with us." That's where a second lieutenant doesn't have much clout. I got into the ambulance. It soon became apparent why they wanted me with them and it wasn't to improve my health. They needed me to direct them to the crash site. The medic opened a bottle of peroxide and poured it over my worst cuts. I showed them the general vicinity where I had come onto the highway. They took a large pair of wire cutters from the crash truck and cut the strands of barb wire and pulled them to one side. Then all three vehicles, the staff car, crash truck and ambulance, took off through the open field.

Another officer was quietly sitting in that crowded ambulance, the Catholic Chaplain who had come along to perform the last rites for the dead pilot.

After the priest performed his ritual, the ambulance crew packed the charred remains of my buddy into the black body bag and loaded it into the ambulance.

A photographer took pictures of the wreckage which was scattered over a wide area. We found my propeller a long way from where I hit the ground indicating that it had sheared off in the air, explaining why my engine stopped so suddenly.

I rode the ninety-some odd miles back to Fort Sumner in the staff car with the pilot instructors with whom I felt more comfortable. Besides there was such a crowd in that ambulance, there was no place to sit. We rolled into the base about 8:30 that evening, twelve and a half hours after I had taken off in that sparkling new P-40. They dropped me off at the hospital where a doctor was waiting to do a little sewing on me.

The next day, Major Jones came to visit me in the hospital. He had flown out to that auxiliary field in one of the AT-6s and waited four hours for me. I explained how our plan had been thwarted. He understood.

An accident investigation board was convened. They examined all of the facts and concluded that the deceased wingman had caused the midair collision because it is always the wingman's responsibility to not crash into the airplane on which he is flying formation.

An ironic note: the young second lieutenant who accompanied the body of my friend back to his hometown for burial, was later killed in the South Pacific, in a midair collision.

The diligent instructors at Fort Sumner had given us their best. We were now qualified fighter pilots ready for combat. One task remained and we would be on our way. We had to take one more six-four flight physical.

That last physical was truly a joke. A few of the older, less dedicated pilots were actually trying to flunk it. A marked contrast to my struggle with that very patient doctor back in Los Angeles. Regardless of their "failing eyesight" and various other complaints, everybody passed. We were given our orders to report to Lincoln, Nebraska, for overseas processing.

106

We were at Lincoln, Nebraska, to be sorted out one more time, to be issued our overseas personal equipment and to be sent on our way to wherever that might be. I wanted to go to Europe. I figured that both the combat and the social prospects would be more promising in the European theater.

We had no idea where we would be sent and our group from Fort Sumner was looking forward to one additional surprise. We would be flying different fighters than the type in which we had trained. P-40s were no longer used by the U.S. combat units. We assumed that we'd most likely get P-51s, which would naturally make us very happy, but if we ended up in P-47s, that would be O.K. too.

The first clue as to our eventual destinations came in the quartermasters warehouse where we drew our personal equipment. Like everything else in the service, we lined up and waited our turn. We watched with considerable anxiety, the goings-on at the head of the line. Some of our buddies came away loaded down with heavy leather flying equipment. To us that meant they were going to England, . . . or maybe the Aleutians.

107

My turn finally came. The man at the counter asked my name. I told him. He looked it up on his list, then disappeared back into the long aisles of racks reaching nearly to the ceiling. The suspense was terrific but it didn't last long. He came back to the counter with his arms full of things for me. They didn't include any leather flying equipment. Instead, I was given one mosquito net, sleeping type, one mosquito net, head type, one bottle of insect repellent, two flying suits, summer type, and the list went on. That was my answer. I was obviously going to the place of my last choice, . . . the South Pacific.

We went by train to Suisun-Fairfield, California, an Air Transport Command base which operated the Pacific flights.

Our flight was scheduled to depart the next afternoon so the little group from Fort Sumner jumped on a bus for San Francisco, fifty miles away.

When we got off the bus at the station in San Francisco, we realized that more than one cab would be needed to get us anywhere so a meeting place had to be agreed upon. We'd meet at the "Top of the Mark" in the Mark Hopkins Hotel.

Three of us, from the last cab, arrived at the Mark Hopkins, got in the elevator and started up for the "Top" to join our friends. As we came out of the elevator, my heart sank when I saw what was taking place. The Top of the Mark had previously experienced some trouble with the law for serving drinks to minors so they were checking everybody's I.D. cards before letting them in and that even included second lieutenant fighter pilots on their way to war. My two buddies pulled out their I.D.s and showed them to the man. He nodded O.K. I thought, what the hell, I'll show him mine anyway. Maybe he flunked arithmetic. He looked at it and said, "Sorry Lieutenant, rules are rules." My two buddies were surprised because I looked older. They went on in to join our group. I headed back to the elevator.

Carrying our two bags of newly issued equipment, we climbed aboard a four-engine Douglas C-54 for the trip west. As we boarded the airplane, we were each given a sealed envelope containing our orders, just like in the movies. I opened mine and read that I was to report to the Fifth Air Force, Combat Replacement Training Center, Nadzab, New Guinea, for P-51 transition and tactical assignment.

The C-54 headed out over the Pacific toward the setting sun. Being the only passengers on board, the twenty-eight P-40 pilots from Fort Sumner had more than enough floor space on which to sleep that night. The fold-down bench seats which lined both sides of the cabin left plenty of room for our baggage, for sleeping on the floor, and for one all-night poker game.

The next morning as we were nearing Hawaii, while gazing out over the blue Pacific, the pilot beside me, a young boy from Texas, commented, "All that water and I can't swim." I don't know how he got through training without being able to swim because we all had to pass swimming tests. Anybody who couldn't pass the test had to take special instructions until they could. He added, "I sure hope the need for me to swim doesn't arise." It didn't. He was killed about a month later on the runway at Clark Field in the Philippines. He was in a formation of landing P-51s. He landed but apparently didn't clear the runway fast enough. The P-51 that landed behind him ran up his tail. His airplane exploded.

After a brief layover at Hickam Field, Hawaii, and two refueling stops, Johnson Island and Tarawa, our C-54 delivered us to Biak, a little island off the northwest coast of New Guinea, just south of the equator. That was the end of their line. Troop carrier C-47s were scheduled to pick us up the next day to take us on the last leg of our journey to Nadzab.

At that particular time, the tiny island of Biak was New Guinea's Grand Central Station. The field was a beehive of commotion. It was end of the line for Air Transport Command Flights. It was head of the line for Troop Carrier flights and it was pickup point for newly shipped-in fighter planes. Troops, ground and air, going and coming, passed through Biak. In spite of the bustling activity, overnight accommodations were minimal. We searched around and finally found the transient officers quarters, a row of tents with folding cots. We supplied our own newly issued mosquito nets. One thing we couldn't complain about was the view. This place had been carved out of lush green jungle on a bluff overlooking the blue South Pacific. Whatever our height was above the water, it was sufficient to provide an elevated view of two P-51s as they gave us a really neat buzz job.

The next morning we hauled our bags and ourselves aboard the gooney birds for the 750-mile flight across New Guinea to Nadzab.

As our C-47 winged its way eastward over New Guinea, taking us to our first combat assignment, this boy, not long out of high school, couldn't help being thrilled.

With our backs to the sides of the airplane, it was easier to just sit in those bucket seats and look over the top of our baggage at the guys on the other side of the airplane, but I couldn't keep my eyes off the window behind my back. This place was right out of the National Geographic, that green rain forest and those mountains, they had to be the Owen Stanley Range that I had read about in school.

First task upon our arrival in Nadzab was to find some living quarters. They had a permanent tent city for the transitioning air crews. All we had to do was find a tent, in the officers section, that was vacant. They were the standard sixteen foot square, four man tents. We found one so four of us moved in, but the neighborhood had already gone to hell. We discovered that many of the adjacent tents were occupied by bomber pilots, bombardiers and navigators. We could always pick out the navigators because whenever they went to the flight line, they took along their little wooden boxes, containing their sextants. The bomber section at Nadzab was flying the four-engine B-24 Liberators, which carried about a ten man crew. The enlisted air crew members lived in another little tent community off to themselves. Among all these new faces were a few old ones, guys whom we had known as fellow cadets in classification and preflight. Some of the bomber pilots had been with us in primary and basic. Generally speaking though, we had very little to do with the bomber boys. We all stuck pretty much to our own little groups. Even if the men in the next tent were fighter jocks, that didn't mean we had to associate with them. If they were P-47 or P-38 drivers,you left them alone. You felt sorry for them but you left them alone. They in turn felt sorry for us. To be a good fighter pilot, you had to believe completely in yourself and in your airplane. They naturally thought theirs were the best just as we knew ours was. This rivalry between the three groups was very spirited, both on the ground and in the air. We called their P-47 Thunderbolts, "Jugs", because they were huge, bulky, heavy and actually looked like jugs. We called the P-38 Lightenings, "Eggbeaters", because their propellers rotated in opposite directions. They sarcastically referred to our beautiful Mustangs as "Spam cans" because the P-51 cost our government much less per airplane than either the P-47 or P-38. In our hearts we knew that the other pilot's airplanes were superb, and although we'd never admit it, we'd love to get our hands on the other airplanes just to find out what they were really like.

Our checkout in the P-51 consisted of reading the manual and spending some time in the cockpit to make sure we knew the location of all the switches, knobs and levers. Then we took it up for a flight.

I taxied out and stopped short of the runway to go through my pre-takeoff checks. Holding the brakes with toe pressure on the rudder pedals, I ran the engine up to 2300 RPM, then I pulled the propeller control knob back until it dropped 300 RPM, then I advanced it to its full forward position. I checked the magnetos, switching from both to left, back to both, then to right, then back to both again. All twenty-four spark plugs were doing their job. One more quick glance around the cockpit. All three internal fuel tanks were full, the selector valve was on left main. Rudder trim was set at six degrees right, elevator trim was three degrees nose-down, and the aileron trim was at zero. Oil and coolant radiator doors were open, mixture control: auto rich, fuel boost pump: on, altimeter on field elevation, directional gyro set to magnetic compass, canopy closed and locked. That was it, but it seemed too simple. I must be forgetting something. Better check again. I did one more fast visual around the cockpit. I couldn't sit there all day so I called the tower and pulled out and lined up on the runway. My left hand moved the throttle forward to the wire. There was a safety wire across the throttle track, near the forward end. When the throttle was against that wire the engine was delivering full "military power". When the throttle was jammed full forward, breaking through the wire, the engine was delivering "war emergency" power. Whenever a P-51 came back with that wire broken, the engine had to undergo a complete tear-down inspection. The engine would only last a very few minutes at the war emergency setting.

I glanced at the manifold pressure. The needle was resting at 61 inches of mercury, the RPM needle was at 3000. That twelve-cylinder Rolls Royce Merlin, built in the United States by Packard, was developing nearly fifteen-hundred horsepower. The big eleven-foot-two-inch diameter four-bladed prop gobbled up huge chunks of the thick jungle air. It lifted off smartly. I reached down and moved the landing gear handle to its up position, just like in the AT-6, none of the physical gymnastics that were required in the P-40. I eased the throttle back to 47 inches of mercury and pulled the prop control back to 2700 RPM. The needle on the airspeed passed 250 miles per hour and was still moving upward. After 285 hours in P-40s, the basic handling of the P-51 was a snap. My concern on that first flight was that I surely must be forgetting something. The feeling was prompted by the fact that I hadn't done anything. I was just sitting there. I looked around the cockpit, mixture control: auto rich, oil and coolant doors: automatic position. There was nothing for me to do except sit there and aim the airplane. There was no doubt about it, the P-51 was a gigantic leap ahead of the old P-40, both in human engineering and aerodynamic performance. After a thoroughly enjoyable familiarization flight, I returned to the field and landed. I was now a qualified P-51 pilot.

We had to get a little time in these new airplanes but rather than just letting us go up and aimlessly bore holes in the sky, they frequently assigned us to fly airdrome defense. All this really meant was that, while we were up there boring holes in the sky, we were supposed to be on the lookout for enemy aircraft. If we ever spotted any, we were expected to intercept them and of course shoot them down. By this time, the real combat fronts were a long way from Nadzab, but we weren't about to question orders. I'd go up and tool around in the sky for the allotted time and I'd dutifully look for enemy aircraft. While circling around high above Nadzab, I'd look and look, hoping to find an airplane sporting the red meatballs. My P-51 and I were itching for a fight. This was only my second flight in a P-51, but I already felt at ease in it and figured I was ready to take on any enemy.

Coming down was fun. I had lots of speed with which to play. This translated into one aerobatic maneuver after another. While still some distance from Nadzab, a thought crossed my mind. I had seen airplanes buzz the field so it must not be against any regulations. So why not give it a try?

I called the tower. "Nadzab tower, this is Peter five one, number so and so, ten miles north, requests permission to buzz the runway." The tower came right back, "Permission granted. Approach from the north. No other traffic at this time." Rolling over into a dive, I acknowledged, "Peter five one, number so and so, roger." As I dived toward the deck, I kept glancing at my airspeed indicator. I got the needle right up to the red line at 505 miles per hour. I was already on the deck before reaching the field so the people on the ground wouldn't know I was coming. I kept the throttle wide open to hold my 500 miles per hour as I went across the field within at least fifteen to twenty feet of the ground. I pulled the stick back sending my airplane up into a huge half loop. I rolled out at the top and asked the tower for permission to land. That was really fun, and to think that it was perfectly legal. Being able to do things like that was a fringe benefit of flying overseas in a combat zone.

The P-51s were a delight to fly but during those first few hours, we did have one problem — a rash of blown tail wheel tires. After rereading the aircraft's manual, we discovered why. We were taxiing the P-51s just as we did the P-40s and even the PT-19s. We had to see past the airplane's nose so instead of taxiing in straight lines, we constantly turned back and forth. This was the way we had been taught — to "S" while taxiing. We were also taught to hold the stick back while taxiing to keep from nosing up and nicking the prop cn the ground. In our first hasty reading of the P-51 manual, we missed the part which explained that the tail wheel would lock when the control stick was full back. To make sharp turns while taxiing, the stick must be held forward of neutral to unlock the tail wheel and allow it to swivel. No wonder we were blowing our tail wheel tires.

All of our combat preparedness training at Nadzab wasn't conducted in the air. One course was taught on the ground, a three day jungle survival course taught by the Aussies. The first day was a lecture which they conducted on the outskirts of our camp. We sat on the ground while the Aussie instructors told us the basic things we should know to help our chances of surviving in the event we went down in the jungle. The second and third days were actually spent in the jungle. As far as I was concerned, the tent that I lived in was as close to the jungle that I cared to be.

Carrying our mosquito nets, a bottle of insect repellent and a few packs of processed food (K rations), we climbed aboard the trucks for the trip into the jungle.

The trucks took us a couple of miles into the jungle, to the end of the road. We climbed out and in single file, followed the Aussie guides into a world that was completely foreign to me. It was a memorable experience and to me a very costly one because I'm sure that it was on this camp-out in the jungle that I contracted malaria which bothered me for many years to come.

Trees hundreds of feet tall with long dangling vines completely screened out the bright noonday sun. The perpetual darkness combined with the incessant noise from the numerous wild creatures magnified the eeriness of this awesome place. Occasionally, the Aussie instructors would stop to show us things which they felt we should know about. They would point out things which were eatable and they would point out things which were poisonous. They mentioned a general rule that if it was red, it was poisonous, but there was one exception. Small tomatoes grew wild in that jungle which looked and tasted just like the tomatoes back home. Walking along through the jungle, I couldn't help but think of the legendary Stanley and Livingston who explored these jungles many years before.

We eventually came to a place which the Aussies decided would be our campground for the night. With machetes, we hacked down a large amount of bamboo and under the supervision of our guides, fashioned a crude sort of shelf on stilts which would be our community bed. Over this we jury-rigged a very crude bamboo roof, on which to hang our mosquito nets. With the construction of our sleeping quarters completed, we dined on the terrible K rations and then bedded down for what turned out to be a truly grim night. No one slept more than a few minutes at a time because of the strange sounds from the jungle's night creatures and the constant attack of the mosquitoes, even inside our nets. The insect repellent was ineffective because our continual perspiring just washed it away. In spite of the heat and humidity, we didn't dare take off our clothes. We just laid there fully clothed in our khaki shirts and pants. We even kept our shoes on. To deprive the mosquitoes of as much skin as possible, we wore white cotton gloves, the same kind with the blue tops that people wear when working in the garden. But the mosquitoes still had a field day. We were literally covered with welts. I had two bracelets of mosquito bites on the gaps of bare skin between my shirt cuffs and the tops of the gloves.

When the pitch black of night gave way to the perpetual twilight of the jungle day, we rolled up our mosquito nets and wearily but anxiously started on our trek out of that miserable place. This was the land of malaria, elephantiasis, beriberi, jungle rot, dysentery and a whole host of other diseases, most of which had no cures. Where there wasn't jungle, there was six-foot high kuni grass which harbored disease-carrying ticks and who knows what else. The rivers and streams were infested with flukes, snakes and a few other deadly creatures. And the surrounding oceans were full of man-eating sharks. For a young pilot who wanted to do his fighting in the skies over France and Germany, this was not the place to be.

Highlight of our training flights at Nadzab were the actual combat missions which we flew to Wewak and Rabaul. Most memorable of these first combat missions was the one led by Lieutenant Colonel Gerald R. Johnson, one of the South Pacific's leading aces. He had shot down twenty-two enemy aircraft.

We listened intently as he briefed us for the mission. We were going to bomb and strafe enemy positions at Wewak, a Japanese holdout on the northern coast of New Guinea, about 260 miles from Nadzab. There would be twelve P-51s in the formation. Colonel Johnson was number one. I was to fly number three in the second flight. He said, "We'll take off in formations of twos. I'll make a wide turn to the left so everybody can join up. En route, we'll fly at about five thousand feet. When we get there, the second and third flights will drop back for spacing. We'll drop our bombs on the first pass then we'll circle, out over the water, and come back for one long strafing pass. Hit anything you see but watch out for the airplane beside you. After we come off the target, we'll join up again over the water and head for home. If anybody gets hit and has to go down, try to make it to the ocean. You'll have a better chance of getting picked up. Now when we get back to the field, if we have enough fuel left, we'll give the ground personnel a real show. You know, they work long hard hours and the only flying they see are a bunch of takeoffs and landings, so today we'll show them a little more. Any questions? O.K., Let's go." Carrying our heavy parachutes with dinghy and jungle pack, wearing our Mae Wests and 45 automatics, we headed for our P-51s.

Even our takeoffs were a pretty good show. This man flew with class. He and his wingman went out a ways on the runway heading and then started his turn so the rest of us could turn shorter and catch up, but he stayed fairly low and turned rather tight, forcing the rest of us to do the same, adding a little something extra to a routine formation takeoff.

We settled down on course at five-thousand feet for the 260 mile run over to Wewak. Below us was a solid green carpet, the hostile jungle of New Guinea. I thought to myself, this was where a P-38 would be pretty nice. If one engine quit, the other one would keep you in the air. Parachuting into that jungle would be a treacherous undertaking. Parachutes would catch in the tall trees and leave the pilots dangling in the air high above the ground. When they unfastened their harness and dropped to the ground, the fall could easily break a leg or an ankle. If a pilot had to go down in this area, he should try to make it to the plains which were covered by the six-foot-high grass. But being spotted by any search and rescue flight would certainly be tough.

We had been briefed on a new rescue technique which was supposedly available to airmen down in the plains area of New Guinea. It was a wild concept but if it worked, who cared. Presuming that they could locate the downed airman, an airplane would fly over and drop the paraphernalia consisting of two long bamboo poles, nylon rope, and a special harness. They also included an instruction sheet explaining how to set it up. The nylon rope formed one large loop stretched between the tops of the tall bamboo poles running back on the ground to the harness which was positioned along the centerline between the two poles. After the downed airman supposedly had time to erect the device, a specially equipped C-47 would arrive on the scene, line up on the two poles and make a low slow pass while trailing a nylon rope with a hook on the end of it. As the C-47 would pass over the two bamboo poles, the hook would pick up the nylon rope stretched between the poles and literally snatch the airman, sitting on the ground in the harness, right into the air. While the C-47 climbed back up, the airman would be trailing behind at the end of the long nylon line. A winch on board the C-47 would reel him in to the airplane. That would be quite a ride but it gave us hope that if we did go down in the jungle, there might be a chance of getting rescued.

Our formation arrived over Wewak. We slid into string formation and in follow-the-leader fashion, we rolled over and descended on the beleaguered pocket of bypassed Japanese. We released our bombs, pulled out and headed for our rendezvous out over the water. We then circled back, in flights of four, and made one long strafing pass across the entire length of the former Japanese stronghold of Wewak. We had been warned against flying too close to the trees near the target area because the Japanese had a favorite trick of planting bombs in the trees and remotely setting them off whenever a low flying airplane came close by. We didn't see much of the enemy during these attacks. Any of them that were left very wisely stayed in their shelters.

We completed the strike, joined up over the water and turned in the direction of Nadzab. We got back with enough fuel for Colonel Johnson's air show. As we approached Nadzab, he fish-tailed his airplane to signal us to get into string formation. We all dropped back into a single line of twelve P-51s, nose to tail and stepped down to avoid the prop wash of the airplane ahead. We nosed down picking up speed as we streaked across our camp area.

Being the number three man in the second flight put me number seven in this follow-the-leader formation so, in addition to being a participant in the airshow, I was also afforded an excellent view of the show ahead — of the six airplanes in front of me as we did slow rolls along the crest of the hills which surrounded the camp area of Nadzab. We performed over both the airstrip and the tent city nested up by the hills. Our little show had to be impressive for everyone on the ground that afternoon in Nadzab.

We shifted back into our standard four-plane flights, then into a twelve-plane right echelon in preparation for landing. We approached the field at about 250 miles per hour. As our near-perfect twelve-plane echelon passed over the runway's threshold, Colonel Johnson banked and pitched up. At one-second intervals, each of the eleven P-51s followed up into the beautiful fan-shaped pattern. As narrow as the runway was, we staggered our landings; one airplane on the right side, the next airplane on the left side and so on, to expedite getting all of the airplanes on the ground.

For some reason, Colonel Johnson didn't land. Maybe he was too close to an airplane still on the runway. Anyway he went around and squeezed into another spot among the landing P-51s, so the first P-51 from the formation to land and taxi off the runway was Colonel Johnson's wingman. I had just landed and was taxiing back to the parking area when I heard the tower hollering, "Airplane that just landed, expedite your taxiing! Airplane that just landed, expedite your taxiing!" A voice came back over the radio, "Blow it out your ass." Needless to say, that remark upset the man in the tower, who was at most a sergeant. He quickly responded with, "Airplane that just transmitted, what is the pilot's name and serial number?" The answer came back, "Colonel Johnson, AO-634211, and I said, blow it out your ass." There was no further comment from the tower.

We parked our airplanes, had our debriefing and were ready to return to our camp area. Colonel Johnson climbed into the jeep which had been loaned to him during his short visit to Nadzab. He asked us how we were getting back to the camp area. We told him that a truck usually took us back and forth but this time it hadn't shown up. He said, "Climb on, I'll take you back." Nine second lieutenants climbed into and on top of his jeep and we started off down the dusty road toward tent city. We presented quite a spectacle. You couldn't even see the jeep for the pile of guys on top of it. We hadn't gone far before we were stopped by an MP in another jeep. The MP, a corporal, walked up to our jeep and first of all had to give us a salute. Upon seeing the silver leaf on the driver's collar, I'm sure he wished he were somewhere else at that particular moment. He tried to explain that there was some regulation against overloading jeeps. Rank definitely has its advantages. Colonel Johnson said to the MP, "O.K., then, you take some of these officers back to their camp area in your jeep." The MP replied, "Yes Sir!" and saluted. Four of the second lieutenants climbed into the MP's jeep.

A great man and a superb pilot, Lieutenant Colonel Gerald R. Johnson was later killed in a non-combat flying accident.

Being among the first of the old Fort Sumner gang to complete the flying requirements at Nadzab, three of us received orders to report to the 71st Tactical Reconnaissance Group, Fifth Bomber Command, Lingayen, on Luzon in the Philippines. So now with 285 hours in P-40s and 35 hours in P-51s, I was on my way to catch up with the real war.

We packed up and boarded a C-47 for the flight back to Biak, then on up to the Philippines. After stops at Zamboanga and Leyte, we arrived at Clark Field on Luzon, which was the end of their line. The remaining eighty miles up to Lingayen were covered in the back end of a bouncing truck.

We didn't have to ask for directions. Three second lieutenants lugging their bags could only be newly arrived pilots looking for the place to report-in. Seasoned-looking troops pointed the way. We went into the headquarters tent to get our specific assignments. The "Judge" was assigned to the 110th Tactical Reconnaissance Squadron and two of us were assigned to the 82nd Tactical Reconnaissance Squadron. We picked up our bags and set out to find the camp areas of our respective squadrons.

Lingayen was the spot where the allies landed when General MacArthur returned to the Philippines. The Japanese didn't expect the landing here because it was in a bay and much farther north than many other more suitable sites. The fighting was fierce but brief. The Japanese airstrip, just outside the town of Lingayen, was quickly taken. Perforated steel mats were laid on the bombed-out runway and the 71st Tactical Reconnaissance Group moved in and took up residence.

The two of us trudged over to a little community of four-man tents nestled under the tall palm trees. We were directed to the C.O.'s tent, so we went over to introduce ourselves.

A very young man was standing in the doorway of the tent watching us approach, through the back end of a pair of binoculars. He was looking through the large end which makes everything appear very small and far away. He had no shirt on so we couldn't tell what his rank was. We asked if he was the C.O. He said yes. We introduced ourselves. His name was William Shomo. It was a very low keyed meeting; a far cry from the rigid way we learned to report-in back in cadets. He asked us what kind of airplanes we'd been flying, then he pointed to a tent on the other side of a rice paddy and told us we could move into that one because it had a couple of empty cots.

Something was bothering me. It started when I first read those orders assigning me to the 71st Tactical Reconnaissance Group. The orders didn't read to a fighter group. I was a qualified fighter pilot and I wanted to be in a fighter group, not in a reconnaissance outfit. The 82nd Tac Recon flew P-51s but they weren't called P-51s. They were called F-6s because they carried cameras in the aft section of their fuselage, just forward of the tail. You could tell them from a regular P-51 because their aft fuselage had a little glass porthole, about eight inches in diameter, on the side and one on the bottom for the cameras to shoot through. They still carried six fifty-caliber machine guns, but this outfit's primary mission was reconnaissance. Fighter-type activities were secondary. I soon discovered that the majority of the pilots had gone through a special kind of RTU, a photo recon school, at Key Field, Meridian, Mississippi. They had not attended a regular fighter-type RTU. Their specialty was flying straight and level and taking pictures, not shooting down enemy airplanes. There was a paradox though in the fact that my squadron commanding officer became an ace and accomplished a feat which stood alone for fighter kills in a single engagement.

124

Just as in World War I, returning fighter pilots executed the traditional victory roll over their home field whenever they had been victorious in aerial combat. Well that day when Shomo and Lipscomb returned, Shomo came across the runway right on the deck and did one roll, another roll and a third roll. By the time he completed his third roll, he was past the end of the runway so he cranked his P-51 (F-6) around in a wide 360-degree turn and came barreling in again over the runway. By this time everybody thought he was just having a good time because after all, reconnaissance pilots just didn't shoot down enemy airplanes. On his second pass, he did three more rolls, then he racked it around one more time and came back down over the runway. He did one more roll, his seventh, then pitched up, chopped his throttle, lowered his landing gear and flaps. Just as he was touching down, Lipscomb came roaring down over the runway and started rolling, one, two, three; then he pitched up, came around and landed. What a day they had! Between the two of them, they had shot down ten enemy airplanes and they had the subsequent thrill of doing ten victory rolls.

William Shomo and his wingman, Lieutenant Paul Lipscomb, had been on a routine VR, visual reconnaissance, mission in northern Luzon. On these VR missions, the lead airplane would fly right on the deck so the pilot could look for Japanese activity under the trees. The other pilot would follow behind and higher, providing cover for the man on the deck. His job was to look out for enemy aircraft. This one day, they spotted a Betty bomber being escorted by twelve Tony fighters. Shomo and Lipscomb immediately started climbing toward the thirteen-plane formation. With throttles wide open, the two P-51s (F-6s) closed in on the big V formation of Tonys. Shomo motioned to Lipscomb to slide over to the other end of the V. So the two P-51s drew up to the rear of the V formation just as though they were joining up except they each blasted both tail-end charlies right out of the sky. Then all hell broke loose. In less than fifteen minutes William Shomo and Paul Lipscomb shot down ten enemy aircraft. Shomo downed six of the Tonys and the Betty bomber while Lipscomb polished off three of the Tonys. Three of the Tonys managed to escape. For his outstanding achievement, Shomo was awarded the Congressional Medal of Honor. He was the 82nd Tactical Reconnaissance Squadron's only ace. In fact, prior to this momentous day, the 82nd's total number of victories was only something like seven. But the 82nd Tac Recon certainly wasn't short of tigers. One of them lived in my tent. He was a quiet man on his second tour of duty. He had gone through this once and was now going through it again.

When cruising around in enemy territory taking pictures, you expected to be shot at but the chances of not getting hit were in your favor. Some called it fate. Some called it luck. Others just didn't talk about it. Airplanes did get hit and some pilots did get killed. A few came mighty close and lived to tell about it. One of those lucky pilots lived in my tent.

During a reconnaissance mission over Formosa, his airplane took a direct hit. Shrapnel or a cannon round ripped through one of his internal fuel tanks. Luckily it didn't explode or burn, but the gasoline for his trip home was vaporized into the sky over Formosa. There was no way he could make it back to the Philippines, but not wanting to visit Formosa, he and the formation turned toward the open sea and headed south in the direction of home. They started climbing for two reasons, to give him plenty of altitude for his inevitable parachute jump and to achieve maximum radio range to hopefully reach a surface station which could get a fix on the spot when he went down.

About one-hundred miles south of Formosa, his fuel-starved engine stopped. He pulled the nose up to slow it down and climbed out. It looked to several of the pilots as if he collided with the horizontal stabilizer because just as he left the cockpit, his airplane flipped around and started to spin. Everybody watched as he tumbled toward the sea. Finally his chute opened. The formation continued climbing on its southerly heading while the leader kept on transmitting in hopes that some distant surface station would hear him and get a fix. One month later, that downed pilot returned to the squadron and what a story he had.

He did in fact get hit by the tail. Just as he cleared the cockpit, he saw his horizontal stabilizer coming straight at him. He put out his arm to deflect the blow, which sent him reeling and tumbling end over end toward the sea thousands of feet below.

To prevent our silk parachutes from mildewing in the humid tropical climate, they were frequently aired out and repacked. Consequently, we often flew wearing a borrowed parachute, a parachute whose harness had been specially fitted to another pilot, a pilot who wasn't flying on that mission. As luck would have it, he was wearing someone else's parachute and unfortunately he hadn't been too selective about the size. He was rather short and the borrowed chute was obviously fitted for a much larger man. The opening impact, especially after a long free fall, was quite a jolt even with a good fitting chute. His wasn't. The chest strap and connecting hardware hit his chin so hard it knocked a tooth through his cheek. That gave him something to worry about as he floated down to the turbulent sea.

Part of our getting "dressed" for a mission included, first

putting on our Mae West, the orange inflatable life preserver which went over our head and was tied by straps that went around our waist and between our legs. Next, we put on our parachute ensemble which included our one-man dinghy which was tightly folded into a rock-hard package about fifteen inches square and about eight inches thick which we sat on. A web strap about eight feet long, folded up inside the dinghy package, had a clip-type fastener on its end. Whenever you put on your parachute, you were supposed to clip the end of that web strap to a ring on the side of your Mae West. Then, if you parachuted into the water, you would still be attached to your one-man life raft by the web strap, even though you had freed yourself from your parachute. Well, not only did he have on the wrong size parachute harness, he forgot to accomplish the simple little task of clipping the end of that strap to his Mae West.

He dropped into the ocean and quickly released his parachute harness to avoid getting tangled in the lines as the canopy settled onto the water. But his parachute didn't collapse. Instead it scooted away like a boat under full sail, dragging his still folded-up life raft with it. His only thought was to get that life raft which was drifting away with his parachute. His frantic efforts seemed fruitless. He was gagging and vomiting from the inhaled and ingested salt water, then it occurred to him to inflate his Mae West. He reached down to his waist and pulled the lanyards releasing the contents of the two little CO_2 bottles into his life preserver. That sure made swimming easier. He got to his parachute, ripped open the cover on his dinghy pack and pulled the pin on its CO_2 bottle. The little one-man raft unfolded and swelled up to its intended shape. After a couple of tries, he managed to get into it. When they named them "one-man rafts" they weren't kidding because it was all one man could do to fit in it. You had to sit in it with your legs bent and it was always full of water. He no sooner got in it before it flipped over dumping him head first back into the sea. After getting flipped over a couple of more times, he realized the necessity to take on each wave with adroit seamanship or be tossed back into the sea. Using the little hand paddles, that were included in the raft, he'd square around and paddling furiously, back into each of the never-ending waves.

The temperature dropped with the setting sun and his thin, soaking wet, poplin flying suit provided no insulation. While sitting there awash in his tiny dinghy, he realized that it had been more than twelve hours since he had relieved himself. Sensing the urge, he contemplated how to go about it. He was submerged in cold water that reached nearly to his chest. Having no alternative, he just relaxed and peed, and to his surprise, received a very pleasant reward. The urine warmed up the sea water trapped in his dinghy, which in turn, warmed him a little. He wished he could have peed all night. But the continual exercise of paddling into the huge swells, trying to keep upright, also helped to keep from getting too cold.

The arrival of daylight didn't do much to brighten his spirits. He knew that his chances of ever being found in that vast ocean were very slim. He had flown over it long enough to know that a single man, in a tiny four-foot raft, was virtually impossible to spot from the air, or for that matter even from a surface vessel. After all, the waves were larger than he was. The odds against him ever being rescued were astronomical. As the day wore on, the elements were beginning to get to him. The water, the wind, the sun, the fatigue of no sleep and now hunger and thirst were adding to his misery.

At first he couldn't believe his eyes but then his ears verified the fact that an airplane was approaching. It was a big PBY Catalina flying boat. It circled around and made a pass directly over him, dipping its wings. In all that ocean, a rescue airplane had miraculously found him.

The big lumbering PBY circled around again and acted as if it was going to land, but then at the last minute it pulled up. The same waves that had been pounding him in his little dinghy were apparently too big for the PBY to attempt a landing. It circled around once more and this time dumped out another raft. He frantically paddled over to it and scrambled aboard. It was a much larger inflatable raft, the kind carried on bombers. It could easily hold five men. He appreciated the larger more luxurious boat, but was very disappointed to find no provisions had been included. He expected to find some kind of canned rations and fresh water. He found neither. The PBY departed.

Just because that navy plane found him one day didn't guarantee they could find him again, and he knew it. But now he could at least stretch out and relax in the larger raft which wasn't nearly so vulnerable to the big rollers.

The next day, to his ecstatic delight, a PBY appeared again circling around until they spotted him. And again it lined up, headed into the wind and slowly settled down for a water landing, but just at the last minute they applied full power to the engines and it climbed back up. On closer look, they must have felt that the heavy swells presented too great a risk for a safe landing and subsequent takeoff. They dipped a wing and flew away.

He couldn't believe his eyes and ears but on the next day, another PBY appeared. It immediately set up for a landing. Its wingtip floats had been rotated to the down position. It made one low slow pass then circled around and came back again lower and slower. This time it was surely going to land even though the surface conditions hadn't really improved. The waves were as big as ever but the PBY pilot decided to take the chance. They lost. One of the huge rolling swells claimed the PBY just as it touched down. With her seams ripped, the crew barely had time to get out their own life rafts and emergency rations before it sank.

It might have been a depressing situation for the eight men who had been aboard the PBY but it was a joyous occasion for the lonely pilot who had already spent three nights out there by himself. He was delighted to have the company and enjoyed sharing their food and fresh drinking water. That fourth night at sea was almost a pleasure compared to his first three. The large rafts, carrying the nine men, were all tied together for mutual security.

Late the next afternoon, a large warship appeared on their horizon. It looked like a U.S. cruiser so they took the chance and shot up a flare from their Very pistol. The flare could be seen even in daylight. The ship turned and headed toward them.

Their guess proved to be correct. It was a U.S. man-o-war. The big cruiser drew alongside and took them aboard. But instead of returning them to the Philippines, the cruiser was heading west on a lengthy war patrol along the China coast. It would be carrying nine very happy passengers.

We flew a lot of visual reconnaissance missions up highway five, which was the enemy's main transportation route through northern Luzon. It was kind of exciting flying up the road right on the deck and looking for the enemy hiding under the trees. They were used to us buzzing and strafing anything that moved on that road so they would hide under the trees during the day and do all of their moving at night. These VRs were always two-plane missions so whenever a lot of airplanes were scheduled we knew we were in for something different.

The operations tent was crammed with pilots. Even before the briefing, we knew this was going to be a biggie. The briefing confirmed it. We were going to photograph about a dozen airfields on Formosa. The airplanes carrying the vertical cameras would fly directly over the airfields while the airplanes with the oblique (side looking) cameras would fly to one side of the airfields. We usually didn't know which way our cameras had been mounted until we got to our airplanes and looked through the glass portholes.

Because of the distance involved we would be carrying external fuel tanks under both wings. The officer, conducting the briefing, said something which renewed my desire to get out of that outfit. He said, "When we hit the coast of Formosa, we'll pick up our fighter cover. P-38s of the 49th Fighter Group and P-51s of the 35th will provide cover for us while we're making our photo runs." Hell, some of my buddies from Fort Sumner were in the 35th Fighter Group. They would be flying cover for me while I'm taking pictures. That was a mighty tough mission in more ways than one. The flak was fierce but worst of all was looking up above and seeing those P-38s and P-51s and knowing that there was where I really belonged.

That night, my Fort Sumner buddy and I had a very private discussion. We lived together in the same tent but our flight leader also lived in that same tent and we didn't want this conversation to be heard by anyone else so we took a walk out among the palm trees. We both wanted desperately to get into a regular fighter group where our primary mission would be shooting at the enemy rather than taking his picture. We discussed our chances of obtaining a transfer. I was certain that if we went through normal channels we'd never make it. We had to try something bold. Our only chance would be to go right to the top, to the commanding officer of the entire 71st Reconnaissance Group, which was truly a big outfit. In addition to the two squadrons of F-6s (P-51s), there were two squadrons of F-5s (P-38s with cameras in their noses instead of guns) and a B-25 outfit. We agreed that the next day we'd try to see the top man. If the two of us went in together, who would do the talking? It was decided that I would be the spokesman. That night as I laid on my cot, I rehearsed what I was going to say.

In combat flying outfits, when the pilots aren't flying their time is their own. In fact it really drags. So finding the time to see the number one man was not a problem.

We went into the group headquarters tent and walked over to the adjutant, who was a major, and asked permission to see the Colonel. He asked us what it concerned. I told him that it was a personal matter. The Colonel had a closed office. The adjutant knocked on his door and went in. He came out and told us we could go in.

We walked up to his desk and gave him a salute. He returned it and said, "At ease. What is it that you want?" I started in just as I had rehearsed, "Sir, all of the pilots in the 82nd Tac Recon Squadron had attended a special reconnaissance school back in the states. We attended a fighter training school. Therefore, if it is at all possible, we would appreciate being transferred to a regular fighter group. It's not that we don't like our fellow officers. They are a fine bunch of men. We simply want a chance to perform the function for which we were trained." The first thing the colonel said was, "Have you made this known to your squadron commander?" I answered, "No sir." He replied, "I suggest you do and in the meantime, I'll see what I can do. Leave your names with the adjutant." We thanked him, saluted and left.

While walking back to our camp area, we discussed the problem of telling our C.O.. We knew that if we had initially gone through proper channels, there wouldn't be a chance of getting a transfer. No officer is going to go to his superior and admit that somebody under his command wants a transfer. It just isn't done.

To compound our particular dilemma, we didn't really have a squadron commanding officer. Sometime before a rumor made the rounds that, because he had been awarded the Congressional Medal of Honor, Major Shomo was being forced to take a new and safer assignment in FEAF, Far Eastern Air Forces Headquarters. The fact that he was gone most of the time lent credence to the rumor. My buddy and I rationalized that we had already committed the cardinal military sin, we had gone over our C.O.'s head. We felt there was nothing we could do now that would change a thing and besides, who would we tell, Major Shomo wasn't there. We decided to just let things stand "as is ". For the present at least it would remain our secret and the Group Commander's.

The suspense during those next few days was terrific. I knew something would happen but I wasn't sure what. Every time we were by ourselves, I couldn't help but repeat my ever-present thought that there sure were going to be some surprised individuals when the word of our bold move eventually got out. He always agreed.

The moment I had anxiously been waiting for finally arrived. The two of us were summoned to Captain White's tent. He was the squadron's operations officer which was the next position in line of command, directly below the squadron commander. As we entered his tent, he greeted us with, "Well, gentlemen, I guess you know what this is about." We responded that we sure did. He told me to, "Sit over there," pointing to a chair on one side of the tent. Looking at me, he continued in a very cold voice, "I'll talk to you later." He then invited my buddy to sit down in one of two facing chairs. He sat down in the other. His tone of voice was much warmer as he asked my buddy, "What do you want to do?" His answer stunned me. He said, "I like it fine in this outfit and, like I told my flight leader, I'd like to stay here in the 82nd." I couldn't believe what I had just heard. This was the man who went with me to ask our Group Commander for a transfer. This was the man who slept in the same tent with me. Here he was revealing that he had gone to his flight leader, told him what we had done and asked to have his request canceled. It seems that the big surprise was for me. Everybody else knew about it except I didn't know that they knew. That flight leader, with whom he had confided, was also my flight leader and he lived in our very same tent. I sat there stunned as Captain White replied, "That's fine with us. We all like you and we'd like to have you remain in the 82nd." He then turned to me and said, "As for you Wyper, I hope for your sake that your transfer goes through because the C.O. doesn't want you in his squadron after you went over his head." His speaking in third person didn't fool me one bit. Rumor had become fact, Major Shomo was not there. This man, Captain White, was the commanding officer. He looked at me and continued, "If your transfer doesn't go through, you'll be transferred to either L-5s or to B-25s as a copilot." I knew that I had taken a big gamble and I considered the risk well worth the possible reward. He addressed both of us saying, "Until the outcome of this is settled, you're both grounded." We got up and left his tent. As we walked back to our tent, I didn't say a word and he didn't either. I was disappointed, not by the fact that he decided to stay, but by the fact that he was not man enough to tell me.

Somehow I managed to endure two more very anxious days of not knowing what fate had in store for me. I had rolled the dice with everything on the line. Word finally came. My transfer had come through. His did not. He got what he asked for. He was going to stay in the 82nd and I got what I asked for. I was being transferred to fighters. My orders read, "Report to Headquarters, Fighter Command, Fifth Air Force, Clark Field, Philippines."

Upon hearing about my transfer, many of the recon pilots made a point to personally congratulate me. In their hearts, every one of them wanted to be a fighter pilot. I packed my bags and climbed aboard a supply truck that was going to Clark Field.

Modern day wars can't be fought without paperwork and Fifth Fighter Command Headquarters, Fifth Air Force, generated its share. A huge room was filled with desks and people, typing, writing and telephoning. I was directed to "that Major over there". I walked over to his desk, saluted and handed him a copy of my orders. He glanced at it and smiled. I asked, "Have you heard about me?" His smile broadened as he answered, "Yes, I've heard about you." He reached into one of his desk drawers, took out a sheet of paper and handed it to me, saying, "Every fighter group in the Fifth Fighter Command, Fifth Air Force, is on that list. Take your pick." I was overwhelmed. I scanned the list. They were all there; the famous P-38 fighter groups, the P-47 groups and every one of the P-51 outfits. I was like a kid in the candy store. I couldn't make up my mind. I liked the P-51 and saw no reason to change so I concentrated on the P-51 outfits. I eventually narrowed it down to the 35th and the 348th. Both were famous fighter groups. I told the major that I would like to join the

348th. He said orders would be cut to that effect.

The major, who prepared my orders, arranged for a jeep to take me over to the 348th Fighter Group which was based at Florida Blanca.

I thanked the jeep driver and went into the 348th headquarters tent to present my freshly cut orders. They assigned me to the 342nd Fighter Squadron. The officer came outside with me and pointed to the tents of the 342nd. I picked up my bags and trudged off in that direction.

An impressive seven-foot-high sign left no doubt in anybody's mind that this was where fighter pilots lived. It was the squadron's scoreboard. There must have been a hundred and fifty little rising sun flags painted on it with big letters on the top spelling out "342nd Fighter Squadron". I was already proud.

I found the C.O.'s tent and went in to meet my new boss. Major Edward Popek was an ace. He had shot down five Japanese airplanes.

Whenever pilots meet, their first question is always, "What type of airplanes have you been flying?" That question was particularly relevant now because the commanding officer wanted to know what sort of experience his new man possessed. It turned out that I had about as much time in P-51s as they did.

The 348th Fighter Group brought the first Republic P-47 Thunderbolts to the south Pacific and proved the "Jug" to be a formidable weapon against the Japanese airplanes, by running up those huge scores posted in front of each squadron. The 348th had just recently changed over to P-51s.

I sensed a degree of uncertainty in the Major's attitude regarding the fact that I was transferred from another organization to his. Transfers from one group to another were not very common. I was sure he was wondering what sort of an oddball was he getting. I tried to explain that I had requested the transfer because I wanted to be in a regular fighter group, not in a reconnaissance outfit. He welcomed me aboard and told me which tent I could move into. He said there was a cot already made up in that tent, which I could have. I thanked him and picked up my bags.

I located the tent and went in to meet my new roommates. There were the usual four cots, three of which were occupied by captains. The fourth cot had also been occupied by a captain, until the day before, when he was killed. A freak accident claimed the life of that veteran fighter pilot. His engine failed on takeoff and he hit a road grader which was parked right at the end of the runway. Both his P-51, and the bombs he was carrying, exploded.

The three captains extended their welcomes. I started unpacking my things while they continued the task of sorting out their former roommate's belongings. His personal effects would be sent home. The government equipment would be turned back to supply. A few of the personal items which weren't appropriate to be sent home were divided up among themselves. Some of his clothing fell into that category. While they were discussing who was getting what, they asked me what my sizes were, "just for future reference".

News and rumors spread fast in a tightly knit little group of fighter pilots and the addition of the first pilot to ever be transferred into their squadron was no exception. That night, during the evening meal, each one of the pilots made a point to come over and meet me. After dinner, the C.O. invited me over to one of the tents for some drinks. I was reminded though to bring my own canteen cup.

When I arrived, with cup in hand, the party was already

well under way. About ten or eleven men were jammed into the one tent, sitting on the cots and makeshift chairs. They told me to go back to the rear of the tent and pour my own. There were two bottles on the table. I identified the contents of one to be grapefruit juice. The other was as clear as water. I asked what it was. One of the pilots said it was 100-proof alcohol. I must have shown some apprehension regarding drinking straight alcohol because the oldest man in the tent, a gentleman whom I had not yet met, spoke up. He raised his canteen cup and said, "It's the best thing you can drink. It's right out of my medicine chest. I'm your doctor and I prescribe it for all of my patients." He was our flight surgeon. In civilian life he was a practicing M.D. in New Orleans. I poured some alcohol into my cup, added the grapefruit juice and joined the party.

At that particular time the 348th was flying numerous sorties every day in support of our ground troops who were pushing the Japanese back on all fronts in Luzon. On those daily flights to places with names like Ilagan, Nagiulian and Balete, we carried and delivered a variety of ordnance including general purpose bombs, napalm and "Daisy Cutters". They were fragmentation bombs designed to explode about a foot above the ground. They did an excellent job of cutting the grass and anything else in their path, hence their nickname, daisy cutters. Radial grooves were cut into their thick steel casings about an inch and a half apart from nose to tail. Those pre-cut steel bands "cut the daisies" in all directions wherever they went off. A small propeller was mounted on the tip of a foot-long rod which protruded from the bomb's nose. An arming wire, running through a hole in the long propeller shaft, kept it from rotating as long as the bomb remained hung under the wing. Once free of the wing, and its

140

arming wire, the little propeller would start spinning and screw the rod in 120 turns, thus arming the bomb. The long nose rods would hit first, exploding the bombs just above ground level. Maybe it was because of their lethal appearance, I'm not sure, but many of our crew chiefs didn't hang around the airplanes very long when our wing racks were loaded with daisy cutters. Out of courtesy, they would stand on the wing and help us with our shoulder harness but they were always a little faster on these occasions. They would give us their usual "Good Luck", then they would jump down and quickly disappear.

Before each mission, we'd be assigned a code name. We would also be given the code name for the particular ground unit that we were to assist. I never could figure out how the names were selected, but they served their purpose. Sometimes we'd be given names of movie stars, but most of the names were less glamorous. Each pilot in the formation would have his own call sign. The first flight, the first four airplanes, were always called red. So they would be red-one, red-two, and so on, preceded by the code words of the day. The second flight might be green, the third yellow and the fourth blue. If tail-end charlie wanted to talk to his formation leader, if the mission's code name was "hatbox", he'd say, "Hatbox red-one, from Hatbox blue-four".

The VHF (very high frequency) radios in all of our combat aircraft had four push-button channels, A, B, C and D, so you can imagine the congestion on those four frequencies. To compound the problem, there were always the wise guys ready with comments to add. Sometimes we'd hear a distant voice exclaiming, "I've been hit! I'm bailing out!" Then we'd hear a much closer voice, in a cool deliberate tone say, "Rough when you lose." I knew that remark came from one of the pilots in my own formation, but you never knew for sure who it was because everybody was wearing oxygen masks. It might be the guy sitting in that airplane right next to you.

As we neared the target area, our leader would contact the ground forces, using our code name and their code name. It usually went something like, "Hatbox one to Stoneface, over." "This is Stoneface, go ahead Hatbox." "I've got eight mustangs, sixteen bombs and lots of ammo. What's your pleasure?" "Hatbox, from Stoneface, we've been getting heavy mortar fire which we'd like to have you knock out. We'll send over a white phosphorous shell to mark the area. Stand by." We'd circle around overhead, watching for the white smoke. Finally we'd see a puff of white smoke as the shell exploded in the jungle. Then we'd hear, "Hatbox from Stoneface, that's the general area." Our leader would kick his rudders, giving us the fishtailing signal to drop back into a loose string formation. We'd check our fuel tanks, fuel selector valve, reach down and turn on our bomb arming switches, adjust our gunsight's rheostat and flip on our gun switches.

Close-support missions were not without their problems, one being to keep from hurting our own ground forces. We frequently had to start our strafing passes over our side of the lines so that any strays and ricochets would go into enemy territory, but this created another hazard for our boys down there in the jungle. When the P-51's six 50-caliber machine guns were fired, all of the spent shells and interlocking steel clips dropped out of chutes on the undersides of the wings. This tremendous amount of steel and brass rained out of the sky whenever we fired our guns. We would be diving and firing directly at the enemy but our spent shells and clips would be falling on our own troops who would quickly relay their displeasure to us.

In addition to their rifle and small arms fire, the Japanese ground forces were well equipped with machine guns, but they seldom used tracers. They no doubt felt that tracers would reveal their positions, which was absolutely correct. Unless we saw the flashes from their muzzles, we could never tell where the ground fire was coming from. Half the time, we couldn't see what we were shooting at because of the thick trees and foliage, but once in a while an ammo dump or a fuel storage tank would go off, making the trip worthwhile.

To break the monotony of life in our little camp at Florida Blanca, we were given, on a rotational basis, the opportunity to spend a couple of days in Manila. The officers of the 348th had rented an old mansion in Manila which served as our town house. A Filipino family lived in it and maintained it — an essential arrangement because our visits were actually few and far between.

When going to Manila some of the officers would take a jeep, but we did have an alternate mode of transportation which I preferred. Somehow, the 348th Fighter Group had a Douglas C-47 in its possession. Different stories circulated as to how we got it. The one that prevailed was that somebody won it in a poker game. Be that as it may, we did have it and the fighter jocks got a kick out of flying it — at least the short distance back and forth to Manila.

One morning, four of us had to leave Manila and the revelers because we were scheduled to fly the next day. Suffering varying degrees of hangovers, we climbed aboard our personal gooney bird. Schmitty, one of our veteran fighter jocks, who seemed to be feeling better than the rest of us, got into the left seat. Fighter pilots, by nature, have little faith in their fellow pilots' abilities so even with my weak stomach and throbbing head, I maintained an awareness of Schmitty's

143

efforts during the engine starts, taxiing and taking off. He did a commendable job.

Sitting in the empty cabin, except for the other two equally quiet pilots, I leaned back against the side of the fuselage and closed my bloodshot eyes. We had been flying for about five or ten minutes when I opened my eyes and nearly panicked at what I saw. Instead of seeing blue sky out the windows, I saw trees and buildings flashing by. I leaped up and went forward to see what was happening. I wasn't sure whether he had completely flipped or was still drunk, but there he was gripping the wheel with both hands and laughing continually as he guided the big C-47 between the trees, telephone poles and houses.

Occasionally we would go on fighter sweeps but by this time enemy aircraft seldom appeared in the skies over the Philippines. The big action was taking place farther north on the beaches of Okinawa where the army was landing and in the waters offshore where the Kamikaze suicide pilots were smashing into our naval ships.

Word came that we were scheduled to move up to Ie Shima, a tiny island off the northern tip of Okinawa. We eagerly looked forward to seeing some real action.

The logistics of moving about 150 officers, about 400 enlisted men, numerous ground vehicles, about 90 P-51s and their support equipment was no small undertaking. All of our ground vehicles and everything else, except our P-51s, were taken down to Subic Bay and loaded on board a couple of LSTs. LST stood for Landing Ship Tanks, the navy's largest ships that could still drive up to a beach and open their front doors. After giving the "water echelon" a week's head start, the P-51s took off and headed north for the thousand mile trip to our new home, Ie Shima.

Ie Shima is a tiny island in the Ryuku group just northwest of Okinawa. It was pretty flat except for one little hill on the eastern end called the "million dollar hill" because that's what they estimate it cost the U.S., in ammunition, to take it from the entrenched Japanese defenders. Two north-south parallel runways, made of rolled coral, extended from cliff to cliff on the western end of the island. Although the two runways were adjacent to each other, they were operated as two completely independent airfields. In fact they didn't even have connecting taxiways. The taxiways and hardstands (airplane parking spots) for the western runway were to its west and the taxiways and hardstands for the eastern runway

145

were to its east. To separate the traffic, one runway used a right-hand traffic pattern and the other used a left-hand pattern. One of the pilots in our squadron wasn't paying too much attention as we approached the runway in the standard tight echelon, fanned up into the pattern and landed. As he touched down, he noticed that the airplane ahead of him was not the P-51 he had been following. Instead it was a P-47. As he turned off the runway, he noticed that the airplane behind him was also a P-47. The only way he could get back to his parking place was to take off again and land on the other runway. Needless to say, he was one very embarrassed pilot.

We were shown our designated campsite, not far from the spot where the famous war correspondent, Ernie Pyle, was killed.

All hands turned to the task of converting a section of barren land into our new home. Somehow, we always managed to "acquire" enough wood to build floors in our tents. Any additional architectural amenities were up to our own ingenuity. Some of the tents became quite luxurious while others remained very austere. Electric wires were strung from our little portable gasoline powered generator to operate any light globes that could be scrounged. From New Guinea through the Philippines to Ie Shima, light bulbs were always a scarce item. Our most cherished personal belongings were the dilapidated canvas director's chairs, mattress covers (to sleep in), air mattresses to sleep on, and light bulbs.

Once used for their intended purpose, parachutes were rarely put back into service, either because of mildew or damage. Consequently, the used chutes conveniently ended up as attractive and functional secondary ceilings inside the lucky pilots' tents. We had one strung up inside the top of our tent. Plywood panels, from the crates in which our aluminum external fuel tanks were shipped, were nailed together around the sides of our tents to form a sort of wainscoting. That used parachute hanging over my head and those plywood panels around our tent certainly pointed up the manufacturing diversification taking place back home. When staring at the ceiling from my cot, I could read the manufacturer's stamp on the parachute canopy. It was "Fashion Frocks of New York" and turning to my side, I could read the manufacturer's name on the plywood panels from the fuel tank crates, a casket company in Ohio. They obviously knew how to make boxes.

Our first mission to Japan was to bomb and strafe the huge Mitsubishi airplane factory at Nagoya. We would be carrying two 500 pound bombs, one under each wing; no external fuel tanks. The entire round trip would have to be made on our 269 gallons of internal fuel. That decision cost our squadron one P-51 and much anxiety for all of the pilots.

The flight up to Japan was uneventful. The dive bombing and strafing went as expected. There was a lot of antiaircraft fire, but that was to be expected. What we didn't expect was to run out of gas on the way home. We used the maximum range cruising techniques developed by Charles Lindbergh, but even that didn't save one of our P-51s.

While flying fighters on actual combat missions in the South Pacific, the "Lone Eagle" proved that an airplane's range could be considerably extended by using very low RPM settings. This, we did. We would have the propeller pitch knob pulled all the way back, reducing the RPM to somewhere around 1750. The exact setting was adjusted to match the other airplanes. This was accomplished by looking at the airplanes ahead through our own spinning propeller. While looking at their propellers, you'd ease your own propeller control knob, on the throttle quadrant, slightly forward or back until you "stopped" their propeller. When your propeller was turning exactly the same speed as theirs, you could see all four of their blades just as though they were stopped. The four-engine bomber boys used this same stroboscopic phenomenon to harmonize their propellers.

On the way home, abut ten miles short of Ie Shima, Lieutenant Babcock's last tank ran dry. Of all the pilots on that mission, poor Babcock was probably the least fit to challenge the open sea by way of parachute. He had been hospitalized in the Philippines with yellow jaundice and had just been released so he could go with us up to Ie Shima. His appearance told the whole story. He was skin and bones and his skin was yellow as were the whites of his eyes. He was very appropriately tagged with the nickname of "Shaky". Well, poor old Shaky had to go over the side. His chute opened and he floated down to the turbulent sea. Fortunately a navy ship spotted his chute and headed to the rescue.

A couple of weeks later, Shaky returned to camp, wearing shiny black navy shoes and a big smile. The ship that picked him up was a seaplane tender that had put to sea to ride out a typhoon which was on its way to hit Okinawa and Ie Shima. And hit us it did! The tremendous force tore down our tents and wrecked everything that wasn't really secure. It also roughed up the sea and the ship on which Babcock was a guest. The entire ship's crew had warmly adopted the frail little fighter pilot whom they had plucked from the sea. They provided him with new khakis and a pair of brand new black navy shoes.

The typhoon was the worst storm that ship had ever experienced; consequently the entire crew became seasick. But their frail-looking guest felt fine and his appetite was ravenous. It was a paradoxical situation; the entire ship's crew was seasick while the sickly-looking Army Air Corps pilot was not. Sick or not, that crew was to be commended on their hospitality. Even at the height of the storm, the seasick cook would make his way to the galley and prepare meals for Babcock, stopping every so often though to throw up.

The schedule for the next day's missions were usually posted around eleven P.M., so needless to say, all of the pilots stayed up to see if they were flying the next day. All that the lists contained were the times and the names of the pilots, but one glance revealed details that never appeared in type. The number of pilots scheduled told something, but their rank told even more. If the list was headed by a captain and followed by lots of lieutenants, you knew it was going to be a tough mission, probably dive bombing and strafing gun installations. On the other hand, if the list was headed by a colonel and included a couple of majors and several captains, you could bet it was going to be a fighter sweep. They were going out to look for enemy airplanes to shoot down. The traditionally early call times were also posted on those flight schedules. Dawn patrols existed just as much in World War II as they did in World War I. The O.D. (officer of the day) would have the chore of going around to the various tents and waking up each pilot whose name appeared on that morning's mission. After staying up until about midnight to see if you were flying the next morning, finding out that you were and that the wake-up call would be 4:30 A.M., the number of hours left to sleep were few at best and frequently even less because of our nightly visitors.

Being the closest U.S. occupied island to Japan, we were introduced to another experience, nightly bombing raids. Sometimes they would skip a few nights but they apparently kept us their number one priority. By this time, the U.S. Navy had pretty much cut off their sea lanes vital to replenish their gasoline supplies. They were very low on fuel and seldom put planes up to intercept our daily attacks on their homeland. Instead, they chose to use what precious little fuel they could manufacture, to bomb us at night, while we were trying to sleep.

We had radar and we had night fighters, but the Betty bombers managed to drop their bombs on us before our night fighters could get to them. The Marines had one squadron of Grumman F6F Hellcats with airborne radar units mounted on their wings and the Army Air Corps had Northrop P-61 Black Widows. They flew nightly "Snooper" missions over Japan, looking for anything they could knock out of the sky. The Marines did most of the defensive patrolling in our vicinity. The first bunch would take off at dusk and fly out to their designated zones. The only trouble was, they would be orbiting at about 10,000 feet. The Japanese bombers would come in much higher and manage to drop their bombs, turn around and head for home before the F6Fs could get up to their altitude. They usually caught up with them on their way home and blasted them out of the sky, but that was long after they had accomplished their intended mission of bombing our tiny little island.

The manner in which the different pilots reacted during those nightly bombing attacks was very interesting. The ones who had gone to the trouble of digging foxholes beside their tents usually availed themselves of that little bit of added protection. Others stood outside and watched the show. There were some pretty heavy antiaircraft guns on Ie Shima and they all responded during those attacks so there was quite a bit of fireworks to watch. Sometimes the bombers dropped phosphorous aerial bombs which exploded high in the air, turning the night into a white eerie noonday glare, so they could pinpoint their targets. Having already seen the show many times before, the coolest tigers didn't even bother to get off of their cots. To them, all that noise was simply an interruption to their sleep. War was their business, they were dedicated fighter pilots and they planned to be back at work the next day.

The number and types of missions were really picking up. The first and second lieutenants were even getting to fly on some of the fighter sweeps. We'd go up to Japan looking for trouble. If we couldn't find any enemy aircraft, we'd end up on the deck shooting at targets of opportunity. Railroad trains were always good targets. You could hit them from any direction but my favorite type of pass was to come in from the side, at a right angle, start shooting at the last cars, then rolling into a bank, turning toward the locomotive, and firing all of the time. The only problem with this type of approach was you'd be awfully close to the locomotive at the end of the pass. If it was a steam locomotive, which most of them were, the idea was to blow it up. That meant you'd be flying right through the bomb that you just exploded. Amazingly, most of our P-51s survived those missions with relatively few battle scars.

On several occasions we provided fighter protection for "Dumbos". They were special air-sea rescue Boeing B-17 Flying Fortresses which had a good-size boat fastened to their belly. It was a double-ender sort of whaleboat made to carry several men and withstand the open seas. I believe they were about seventeen feet long. The Dumbo would orbit over the water, offshore from wherever a large bombing raid was taking place. If any bombers were disabled to the point where they had to be abandoned, they would try to bail out over the water. The B-17, Dumbo, would then drop its boat. Three parachutes would let the boat float down to land upright in the water. Our job was to do whatever was called for to protect the B-17 and the downed airmen until they could get into the little boat, get its engine started and try to get the hell out of the general area. We always joked about those boats, saying that if they ever dropped one for us, we would get in it and head straight for San Francisco.

During many of our pre-mission briefings, we were shown on the big wall map where one of our navy submarines would be standing by, under the water of course, to rescue us if we went down in the vicinity. We would be given the sub's code name and the radio frequency on which it could be contacted. I guess they would stick up an antenna during the time of our scheduled strike.

Before leaving on the really long missions, the flight surgeon would pass out Benzedrine pills to each of us. I'd put them in my pocket to have them with me just in case, but there was always enough going on to keep me awake without popping the pills.

Flying combat missions over Japan was a tough assignment. We individually tried to mentally condition ourselves for the eventuality of possibly being shot down. It was a very real possibility which did happen to some of our buddies every day. We were shooting at the enemy and they were shooting at us. This is where flying in Europe would have been so much nicer. If you went down there, at least you looked like the natives, but not so with us in Japan. We wouldn't have a chance and we knew it. Every combat pilot must have contemplated the probability of his being shot down and what he would do. You figured if and when it happens, you wouldn't have any time to think it over, so I privately formulated my own advance plan. If my airplane was damaged to the extent that it was going down, I would make every attempt to get it to the water. If I could get it to the water with sufficient altitude, I'd bail out. If it took all of my altitude to reach the water, I'd ditch the airplane and take my chances getting out of it. On the other hand, if I could not make it to the water, I planned to remain in my airplane. If I could guide it, I planned to aim it at the best target I could find.

Somewhat reminiscent of the old seamen's "cup of grog", the Army Air Corps had its controversial ration of "combat whiskey". The regulations authorized every combat air crew member to receive two ounces of whiskey upon his return from a mission. Some organizations doled it out just that way, but not the 342nd Fighter Squadron. Whenever a quantity became available, the bottles were passed out to each of the tents so all of the officers could enjoy it together however they wished. During the dry spells between these shipments of booze, there was always our flight surgeon with his seemingly unlimited supply of 100-proof "medical" alcohol. So there were lots of evening get-togethers. Sometimes they were quiet affairs with just two or three of the officers sitting around in their tent talking about their favorite subject. You might think it was girls but it wasn't. The subject was always flying but sometimes it drifted quite a ways from the reality of the day. One of our much discussed topics was how a fly got onto and off of the ceiling. That much-debated subject was never really settled. Some argued that it did a half roll while others swore that it did a half loop.

The non-flying officers in our squadron were always welcome to our parties. Their functions included the flight surgeon, intelligence, communications, engineering, ordnance and supply. Pilots had some slang expressions for the Air Corps' non-flying officers such as "ground pounders" and "gravel crushers" but these terms were reserved for outsiders, never our own fellow officers.

In spite of the superficial conviviality, psychological barriers did exist between the two groups, between the pilots and the non-flying officers. The barrier was actually manifested by the ground officers. Although their jobs were essential, they didn't share the glamour and the risks of the much younger fighter pilots. They couldn't help but feel like outsiders even though they were always invited to our "auger" parties. During the first few drinks, the conversations would be of mutual interest but as the evenings wore on, only one subject was discussed — flying. They were unintentionally left out. I couldn't help but feel sorry for them.

An interesting insight into one non-flyer's thoughts was revealed one night over a couple of drinks. The squadron intelligence officer, who lived in our tent, told me how he tried to get the feeling of what it must be like for us on our long-range missions. (With external fuel tanks and the cruise control techniques pioneered by Charles Lindbergh, we frequently flew seven and eight hour missions.) His daily job was to give us the latest intelligence information regarding the route we would be flying, enemy air and ship sightings, target information and anything else relevant to the particular mission. At the conclusion of each mission, he would conduct the debriefing and write up the intelligence report. In civilian life, he had been an accountant, a CPA, in Kansas. He would see us off in the morning and then wait for our return late in the afternoon. He said he just couldn't imagine how we could sit in those P-51 cockpits for seven and eight hours. So one day, after we took off for Japan, he returned to our empty tent and sat down in his dilapidated director's chair and stayed in that chair until it was time for us to return. To pass the time, he read a book.

We routinely escorted heavy bombers over Japan, but because of our speed differential, we'd fly by ourselves up to the islands just south of Kyushu to rendezvous with the bombers. We'd take off from Ie Shima in two-plane formations, join up into our squadron formation and head for Japan, four hundred miles to our north. To make it easier on everybody, the leader would call out the power settings to the formation. But even mundane words like, "Foxy red one to formation, we'll climb at forty-six inches and twenty-seven-hundred RPM," drew anonymous comments from some of the smart ass young tigers, comments like, "Well Hot Dog!" or "You don't say." They just couldn't resist the opportunity to mouth-off to their direct superiors with very little chance of ever being detected. With all of us wearing oxygen masks and dark goggles, to cut down the sun's glare, there was no way of telling who had the big mouth.

One morning, we picked up about twelve B-24 Liberator bombers over the Osumi Islands just south of Kyushu and took up our positions weaving back and forth above them. They turned to a northerly heading right up the middle of Kyushu. They were about 12,000 feet and we were at about 14,000 feet which presented us with an added problem. We were flying right at the altitude where our two-stage superchargers automatically shifted from low to high blower. It was distracting enough to have the heavy flak exploding uncomfortably close without having our superchargers kicking in and out. That was one thing I would have changed on the P-51s. It had a toggle switch for manual operation but it was spring loaded. In tight formations climbing to higher altitudes, at about 12,000 feet, the leader would tell everybody in the formation to hold their supercharger switches in the first stage. With one hand, we'd hold it in the first stage until we had passed through 15,000 feet at which time the leader would call to the formation, "So and so, red one to formation, at the count of three, release your switches. One, two, three." The entire formation would leap ahead as all of the second stage superchargers kicked in together. If it was not done that way they would be kicking in at different times because they operated on barometric pressure and no two airplanes were exactly the same. So here we were, weaving back and forth over the bombers, amidst the flak which we could hear and feel, some too close for comfort, and our superchargers were cutting in and out. Every time the second stage kicked in, you'd get pressed back in your seat by the increased thrust. You'd look down at your instrument panel and see the little amber light showing that the second stage was operating. You'd breathe a sigh of relief and just about that time it would kick out. You'd be thrown forward into your shoulder straps. You'd immediately think you'd been hit. Then you'd look down and see the light was off meaning it was back in low blower.

We were on the same radio frequency with the bombers so we could hear their conversations between planes and also some of their intercom talk which indicated they were taking hits and some of their crew members were getting hurt. I was glad to see them finally lined up on their bomb run so we would soon be getting out of there. But to my surprise, they didn't drop bombs. Instead, thousands of leaflets floated out of the bombers. Our air force had started a policy of telling the Japanese in advance when and where they would be bombed next. I'm sure those bomber boys didn't appreciate getting clobbered on that kind of mission.

After their "paper delivery" the lumbering Liberators

turned about 150 degrees and headed back into the heart of Kyushu. Pretty soon they set up for another run, but this time they delivered the real hardware. Hundreds of 500-pounders rained down on the railroad marshalling yard 12,000 feet below. The destruction was awesome.

Living in a day-to-day, life and death sort of world couldn't help but distort your sense of values. This was humorously pointed up one morning while a bunch of us were riding in and on a jeep on our way out to the airstrip to go on a mission. The lieutenant at the wheel was driving kind of wild which prompted another young lieutenant to holler, "For Christ's sake, slow down or we'll all be killed!" Another lieutenant said, "Speed up and maybe we'll have a wreck and I'll break a leg and won't have to fly any more missions." At least he got a good laugh from the rest of us.

There were seventeen names on the mission schedule that morning. A full squadron is sixteen airplanes, four flights of four. But this mission had seventeen pilots scheduled and most of them were lieutenants. First Lieutenant Wyper was number seventeen. I was scheduled as the spare. If one airplane couldn't make it, I would take his place. We knew this was going to be a tough one. The briefing confirmed it. We were going to Japanese-occupied China, past Shanghai and up the Yangtze River to bomb and strafe reported shipping and a heavy concentration of shore-based antiaircraft guns. Our objective was to destroy the ships and to knock out at least some of the shore-based guns.

We were each given a packet containing a silk map of that part of China, silk instead of paper so we could still use it after it got wet, a silk American flag and 50,000 dollars worth of Chinese money for us to buy our way out if we went down. The Japanese obviously paid a bounty to the Chinese for turning over any downed Americans. Hopefully it was less than the

50,000 Chinese dollars that we would have.

We went out and climbed into our airplanes. Under one wing hung a 500-pound bomb. Under the other wing hung a seventy-five gallon fuel tank. We fired up our airplanes and started to taxi out. While the seventeen P-51s were clustered on the taxiway waiting to take off, I heard one of our pilots call the leader, "Buster red one, from buster blue one, my coolant is boiling over." This very seldom happened to our liquid-cooled Rolls Royce Merlin engines (built by Packard) but they did have a soft plug or valve which allowed the coolant to escape if it got too hot. I looked around at the other P-51s and spotted the one. A captain whom I knew very well was sitting there in his airplane with his radiator doors shut which of course overheated his coolant and caused it to boil over. Before we got airborne another pilot called to report the same ailment. Apparently all fighter pilots are not tigers, at least not all of the time. For one reason or another, five of our planes never got off the ground that day.

Twelve P-51s joined up, banked to the left and headed northwest toward China five hundred miles away. The standard procedure after takeoff was to draw fuel from each of our tanks so we wouldn't have any surprises later on. After we had tried each internal tank, the left and right internal wing tanks and the fuselage tank, we would then switch the selector valve to the external tank hanging under our wing. By the time we got to that point, we were a good distance out from Ie Shima. One of the young lieutenants called our leader, telling him that he couldn't draw any fuel out of his external tank. The leader told him to return to Ie Shima, but because we were almost a hundred miles out, he designated another pilot to go with him. That way, if either of them went down, the other would know where. Now our formation had been reduced to ten airplanes. Pretty soon, another pilot called the leader saying that his engine was running rough. The leader told him to go back and to take his wingman with him. Our scheduled seventeen-plane mission had now been reduced to eight aircraft, less than half the number with which we started.

The P-51 was a fine airplane, but it did have one very minor flaw which occasionally caused new pilots to screw up. It turned out that the young pilot on that mission who couldn't draw fuel out of his wing tank was actually trying to draw fuel out of his bomb. The P-51's fuel selector valve, located below the instrument panel between your legs, had five positions on it. Three of the positions were very logical, two were not. When the handle pointed to the rear it was on the fuselage tank which was to the rear, behind your seat. When it pointed to the right, it was on the right internal wing tank and the same for the left internal tank, but "Murphy's Law" was introduced when it came to the external drop tanks. The selector valve had to point to the left to draw fuel out of the right drop tank and had to point to the right to draw fuel from the left drop tank. It was a simple thing to get used to but more than one new pilot had his engine momentarily stop when he tried to draw fuel from the wrong wing station, the one holding the bomb.

We had a unique way of navigating on flights like that when flying over hundreds of miles of open sea to a point on a strange shore. We had no radio navigational aids and the winds aloft reports from our weather forecasters were very unreliable. If you tried to compensate for the wind vectors they predicted, you could really find yourself in trouble. If you flew a course directly to your desired destination, the ever-present winds would blow you to one side of the course, but you wouldn't know which so when you eventually reached the coast, you wouldn't know which way to turn, left or right. Our very simple but effective system of foolproof navigation was to build in a gigantic error, to fly a course far to one side of the planned destination. That way, when we eventually hit the coast, we would immediately know which way to turn to find our objective. In this case our intended checkpoint was Shanghai, so we flew a course which would put us on the China coast well south of Shanghai.

About two hours out, the coast of China came into view. Our eight P-51s banked to the right, to the north, and we started looking for Shanghai and the Yangtze river. We had already emptied our external wing tanks so they would be delivered to the enemy along with our bombs. Sometimes we had shortages of the aluminum wing tanks during which periods we were instructed to bring them back. The only time we'd drop them, under those circumstances, was when we encountered enemy aircraft.

As we were turning inland to follow the Yangtze to our target area, we met a PBY Catalina flying boat heading east toward the open sea. During our pre-mission briefing, we had been told that an air-sea rescue plane would be standing by offshore during our strike. We made radio contact with the PBY only to find out that they were on their way home. Apparently there was some scheduling foul-up because their allotted standby time had expired. They wished us good luck and kept right on going. Well, we had flown a lot of other missions without rescue aircraft standing by so we weren't too upset.

We approached the target area at about 25,000 feet and were greeted by very heavy flak verifying that this had to be the place. I adjusted the light intensity of my gun sight, turned on my gun switches, armed my bombs, positioned my empty fuel tank for release, and waited my turn. The man ahead of me was well on his way so I rolled over and pulled the stick back until I was heading straight down. We did vertical uncoordinated rolls on the way down to increase the enemy's aiming problems. The P-51 far below me pulled out so I could now open fire. My right finger squeezed the trigger. I stopped rolling just long enough to center the ball, line up my sight on the largest ship and press my right thumb on the bomb release button. Mission accomplished. Now to pull out. In spite of the high G forces, I managed a quick backward glance to watch my bomb go off. We started moving back into formation as we raced east towards the coast.

When I drew into formation, I was informed that my empty fuel tank was still on my wing. I said that I would try to shake it off after we got out over the ocean. We leveled off at twelve thousand feet and headed in the direction of home. Navigation would now be critical because we would not be approaching an endless coastline. Instead we were heading for a tiny little island over five hundred miles away.

I pulled out of the formation and tried to shake off my hung tank. This was a fairly common problem. It seemed that the empty teardrop -shaped tanks formed sort of an airfoil which in combination with a tight-fitting bomb rack, had a tendency to defy gravity. In addition to working the electric button, I repeatedly pulled the manual salvo handle. I slowed the airplane down, pulled the nose up and violently kicked the rudder pedals, all to no avail. Here I was sitting up there just off the coast of China, which at the time was occupied by our enemy, doing the very things which would put an airplane into a spin. It wouldn't come off. So I moved back into the formation and we continued on our way.

It took over two hours for us to make the flight from Ie Shima to Shanghai, so being as how we had to rely on dead reckoning, we had to assume that it would take us two hours to fly back to Ie Shima. It had been an hour and fifteen minutes since we departed the China coast. I was squirming around in my seat to get more comfortable for the next hour when I looked down and couldn't believe my eyes. There was Ie Shima. What a delightful surprise.

Another squadron in our group flew the same mission that day, but at a different time. They weren't as lucky as we were. They flew out their ETA (estimated time of arrival) and saw nothing on the horizon except ocean. Their leader was confronted with a very tough decision. If the wind at their altitude was from the east and they made a one-eighty, they would end up back in enemy territory. If the wind was from the west and they kept on their easterly heading, they would end up far out into the Pacific. Looking down at the whitecaps, he decided that the wind must be from the west so he turned the formation around and headed back into the afternoon sun. With their fuel running dangerously low, he started transmitting for a fix. He finally made contact with Okinawa and received a heading which wasn't many degrees from the direction they were flying. He had made the right decision.

We approached our runway in the usual tight, smart-looking echelon and pitched up and out into the standard fan-shaped landing pattern, lowered our landing gear, flaps and landed. After landing, I learned that my hung wing tank came off just as I pitched up out of the echelon. It landed in an enlisted men's camp area but miraculously missed all personnel and their tents. It certainly was not my intention to fly thirteen hundred miles and then return home to "bomb" our own troops.

As might be expected, Ie Shima in 1945 offered very little in the way of recreational activities. There were the "auger" parties during which time a few of the participants actually augered in. One of those parties produced another bizarre byproduct — a drunk driver. As small as the island was, one of the young tigers got tanked up and managed to go out and pile up a jeep. He was not seriously injured but his future paychecks reflected numerous deductions to reimburse Uncle Sam for the jeep.

163

Most every group of servicemen had a mascot of some sort and the 342nd Fighter Squadron was no exception. Our animal retinue included a big female English bulldog named Banzai, another big old mongrel and a little spider monkey, irreverently named after the Japanese warlord Tojo. Banzai and Tojo didn't get along too well. They were normally kept apart but one day the big old English bulldog just about had herself one little spider monkey.

Banzai had recently given birth to a litter of very cute chubby half-English bulldog puppies. One day, to keep them from wandering off, they had been placed in a shallow foxhole beside one of the tents, but through somebody's oversight, that particular foxhole was within Tojo's reach. The little spider monkey was about a foot high but his waist was small enough for a cloth wristwatch band to serve as a belt to which a fifteen-foot nylon cord was tied. The other end was tied to a tent stake which gave him a combat radius of fifteen feet, including access to the foxhole containing the puppies. Several of us witnessed the ensuing altercation.

Banzai was not around so Tojo took advantage of the situation to entertain himself by tormenting the little puppies. He was kneeling down by the edge of the foxhole and, with one of his long arms, was poking the little puppies who were unable to escape. Well, it wasn't long before Mama heard the yelps from her little offspring and came charging to the attack. Tojo scurried for his life up the rope from the stake to the tent and on up the tent to the end of his fifteen-foot leash. With his nylon cord pulled taut, little Tojo was sitting terrified on top of the tent. Banzai grabbed the nylon cord in her teeth and started pulling him down off of the tent. After waiting as long as we dared, in hopes of teaching him a lesson, we interceded to save his life. But unfortunately he was to live only a couple of more weeks.

His nylon cord leash was tied to one of our washstands, a rickety structure about four feet high holding an inverted steel helmet which served as a washbasin. Apparently he circled the stand too many times in one direction, wrapping all fifteen feet of his cord around it and somehow pulled it over on himself. Having nothing better to do with their idle time, a couple of the officers started planning an elaborate funeral and burial for little Tojo.

One of the administrative officers wrote a fitting eulogy. Somebody else built a suitably-sized little pine box. A hole, about one foot long and a half-foot wide, was dug and everybody was invited to attend. We didn't have a chaplain so the author read his eulogy; then the wooden casket was lowered into the grave by gauze strips acquired from the Doc's medical supplies. The grave was covered and a simple wood marker was put in place containing the inscription, "Tojo, killed in action, July 15, 1945".

When not flying, time was always a drag. Dogeared books were read and passed on, letters were written, lots of cards were turned and many I.O.U.s were signed. One of the young pilots in our squadron undertook a more challenging form of diversion. He started to build a sailboat.

Singlehanded, he was transforming a junked 300-gallon wooden P-38 belly tank into a recognizable little boat, but no one project probably ever had more critics than Lieutenant Henry's sailboat. After the evening meal, the critics would gather around the little boat setting beside Henry's tent. Everybody had suggestions to offer. Their general consensus was, "It will never work." Others freely gave specific suggestions. Henry was beginning to have doubts himself. Having done a little sailing myself, and noticing that it was big enough to hold two men, I offered my services to become a partner. He accepted and I pitched in. A considerable amount of work had already been accomplished but a lot still remained to be done. He had cut off the pointed tail of the molded plywood teardrop-shaped tank and installed a very smart-looking boat-type transom. He was busy sealing the joints around the centerboard well which protruded up into the cockpit.

Although it ended up with most of the standard sailboat components, the overall appearance wasn't exactly conventional. This was mainly because the hull started out as a 300-gallon drop tank for a P-38, not a two-man sailboat.

From wrecked airplanes, we were able to salvage everything we needed except the mast and the sails. We couldn't find anything suitable for the mast so we ended up building one. We obtained two long strips of wood about three-quarters of an inch thick and joined them together in a T-shape with lots of screws. The parachute riggers cut some old damaged cargo parachutes to our specifications and sewed hems, pockets for battens, and all of the attaching points. A wrecked Curtiss C-46 cargo plane provided the stainless steel cables and turnbuckles for our stays. From a wrecked P-51, we scrounged the steel armor plate which was mounted behind the pilot's seat. After a little cutting with a welder's torch, it was transformed into our centerboard keel. The rudder was cut from another rustier piece of sheet steel. The hydraulic wobble pump handle from a wrecked B-24 made a perfect tiller.

Throughout the entire project, our many critics continued with their unending flow of suggestions. Some of those young pilots had never even seen the ocean before entering the service, but to hear them talk you would have assumed they were all graduate marine architects with vast sailing experience. They told us what was wrong with it, why it wouldn't work and what we should do to improve it. After looking at it for a while, one pilot flatly told us that the mast was too tall. After that very authoritative piece of information, Henry was ready to cut a few feet off the mast. I told him to relax and just continue what we were doing at the time. The very next man to drop by looked at it for a while, then informed us that the mast was too short.

The big day finally arrived. Our many critics were all on hand to witness what they considered would be an inevitable catastrophe. The six-by-six truck, carrying our boat, was followed by a convoy of jeeps loaded with skeptics as we set out for the island's only sandy beach.

We lifted it off the truck and carried it down to the water's edge, put the mast in place, fastened the stays, tightened the turnbuckles, clipped on the jib and mainsail, then pushed it out into waist-deep water so we could hang the rudder and lower the centerboard. The two of us jumped in and hoisted the mainsail. Being the only experienced sailor, I took the helm with mainsail sheet in one hand and tiller in the other. Henry raised the jib and pulled it taut. We were fully underway sailing southward with the wind, away from the beach and the small gathering of critics. Our little craft was performing beautifully. The disappointed skeptics climbed into their jeeps and went back to camp.

About three-quarters of a mile out, we turned around and started tacking back toward the island. Not wanting to usurp the controls because Henry had done the majority of the work, I suggested that we trade positions. He took over the mainsail and tiller and I moved forward to handle the jib.

Both of us were on the high side of the boat as we tacked

toward shore. Henry was holding the main in close which laid the mast over quite a ways like any good sailboat pointing to windward, but because our boat was so small, things happened extremely fast. We were heeled over just far enough to take water into the cockpit over the low side. I told Henry to let go of the mainsail, but in that split-second, enough water came in to lower the boat so that the top of the centerboard well was below the outside water level. As I saw water starting to flood in through the opening at the top of the centerboard well, I leaped over the side and told Henry to do the same. I was hoping to lighten it enough to put the top of the centerboard well back up above the level of the ocean but it didn't happen. She was going down. We had one item in the boat that would float, a bright yellow seat cushion which had been equipment on a large aircraft. I grabbed the longest rope and quickly tied one end to the mast and the other end to the yellow cushion. That little foot-and-a-half-square yellow cushion bobbing on the surface marked the spot where our boat was resting on the ocean floor.

Fortunately, most of the skeptics had already left the beach and gone back to camp, but the few that remained saw exactly what they had come to see. They figured it wouldn't work and as far as they were concerned it didn't. They saw it sink. Henry and I had a long way to swim but we were in no big hurry to meet the "I told you so" crowd so we took it easy and conserved our energy. It was no use trying to explain what actually happened. Our little boat worked fine, it just had limitations and required quicker reactions than we had anticipated.

That evening, Lieutenant Henry and I climbed into a jeep and set out to track down the outfit that operated the ducks, the amphibious boat/trucks that were used to bring in supplies from ships anchored offshore. Ie Shima had no harbor so everything had to be brought ashore by these amphibious vehicles called ducks. We located the outfit's commanding officer, a captain, who probably already thought that pilots were a little strange. I'm sure that we removed any doubts that he may have had. We tried to explain that we had a little sailboat that was resting on the ocean floor about three-quarters of a mile offshore, and that the exact spot was conveniently marked by a buoy. We suggested that if he would be kind enough to loan us one of his ducks, we figured we could pull our boat to the surface and bring it ashore. He made one available to us along with a driver.

Another pilot in our squadron, also named Henry, was an experienced skin diver so we invited him to join us on our salvage operation.

We directed the driver to the general area and sure enough, there was the little yellow aircraft seat cushion bobbing up and down right where we had left it the day before. The plan was to take down some heavier ropes and tie them to our sunken boat so we could pull it up to the surface. Henry, the expert swimmer, and I dived over the side. I followed him down by simply going hand-over-hand down the line which was still tied to the cushion. I got down to the top of the mast but the pressure caused my ears to ache so I retreated to the surface. Henry managed to get a heavy rope tied to it, then the four of us, the two Henrys, the driver of the duck, and I, pulled it up to the surface. We secured it to the side of the duck and headed for the beach.

The only thing lost was the rudder and tiller so we had to scrounge around for material to make a new one. We also added another innovation. We figured if more space was filled with lightweight air tanks, less space would be available for water, so it might not sink next time. From wrecked bombers, we obtained several large low-pressure oxygen tanks, which we sealed and mounted inside the bow and stern compartments. Our second launching was uneventful. We had a neat little boat which helped pass many an otherwise dull afternoon.

In the states, army chow never won any culinary awards and overseas it was the undisputed worst of all the services. Our very limited menu was dehydrated, powdered, condensed and canned, but a couple of us discovered a way to indulge in a pleasant respite from the consistently atrocious food.

A Seabee outfit was based on the island, so knowing how well the Navy traditionally ate, another lieutenant and I decided to try and sneak into their messhall to at least, for once, have a decent meal.

That evening, we 'forgot' to put the bars on our collars and the silver wings on our shirts, so wearing just plain khakis, we strolled into their Quonset hut along with the sailors, picked up a tray, went through the cafeteria-style line, sat down at one of their tables and had ourselves a meal like we had not tasted since leaving the states. There was no doubt about it, when it came to food, the Navy certainly took care of their own and that one evening, they unknowingly took very good care of a couple of scrawny Army Air Corps fighter jocks.

Being on the closest base to Japan guaranteed a variety of exciting missions. We never knew for sure what to expect until the pilot briefings just before takeoff. One morning we were told that some enemy warships had been sighted at Japan's big naval base at Sasebo, on the northwest coast of Kyushu. We would be carrying one 500-pound bomb and one external fuel tank. After that first mission from Ie Shima up to Nagoya, we always carried at least one external fuel tank.

The captain, who was going to lead the mission, took over the briefing after the intelligence officer's report on the ship sightings. He told us what altitude we would fly to Sasebo and how we would attack, depending what was there. If the report proved to be incorrect, which sometimes happened, we would bomb an alternate target and then strafe targets of opportunity before coming home. Speaking of targets of opportunity, probably the most shot-at objects in all of Japan were the lighthouses on their inland seas. I'll bet every U.S. fighter pilot peppered at least one lighthouse during his missions over Japan. We would be roaring along right on the water looking for boats to shoot at when all of a sudden we'd see a lighthouse up ahead. The white cylindrical towers protruding out of the water all by themselves were irresistable targets.

Our flight approached Sasebo at about 20,000 feet. This was one of their main naval bases but our heavy bombers had previously done a good job of reducing its operational efficiency. There were definitely a couple of ships down there. One was very large and partially covered with camouflage netting. Our leader fishtailed, giving us the signal to spread out for the attack. One by one we rolled over and dived toward the largest ship. An impressive array of guns responded to our attack. Then we saw what it was — a full-sized aircraft carrier. Several good hits were scored including what appeared to be one bomb, by our leader, right down its stack. We fired our guns during the dive, before releasing our bombs, but that was all the strafing they were going to get from us that day. Their automatic cannon fire was about the heaviest we had ever encountered. We considered ourselves hotshot fighter pilots, but not kamikazes.

During those last weeks of the war, enemy aircraft became very scarce even over Japan. They had a shortage of fuel, pilots and airplanes, and what they did have, they were saving for their final stand to try and ward off the inevitable invasion of their homeland. Whenever they did venture aloft, their survival rate was extremely poor. On August 1st, 1945, Colonel Bill Dunham, from group headquarters, and our squadron commander, Major Edward Popek, each with a wingman, were prowling around over Japan on a fighter sweep when they happened upon the very sort of scene they were looking for.

They were cruising at about 17,000 feet over the southern coast of Kyushu when they came upon about eighteen Japanese fighters attacking a formation of B-24s. The four P-51s already had a couple of thousand feet altitude advantage so they immediately dived into the melee. Colonel Dunham and his wingman, Lieutenant Tom Sheets, knocked down two of the enemy aircraft and Major Popek shot down two. That was the best they could do because while they were knocking down those four airplanes, the other fourteen were hastily departing. Colonel Dunham was already a three-time ace with sixteen victories and Major Popek had long been an ace with five previous victories.

Another tough assignment was to knock out as many antiaircraft guns that we could, around the tunnels at Yawata. It seemed that they had undersea tunnels connecting Kyushu to Honshu, which were scheduled to be bombed by our B-29s. So to reduce the number of B-29 losses, fighters would be sent in ahead of the B-29s to bomb and strafe the antiaircraft gun installations.

As we were climbing into our airplanes that morning, I noticed the all-too-common sight at the end of the runway, the telltale pall of black smoke, a familiar sight at all combat air fields. Whenever you saw it, you knew that somebody went in on takeoff. I had already seen several columns of black smoke

173

off the bluff end of our runway at Ie Shima, but this morning it had a special significance. I asked my crew chief if he knew who it was.

It was "Ace" Parker, a famous test pilot from the Republic Aircraft Factory. He was taking off in a P-47N, Republic's largest Thunderbolt (Jug) to demonstrate both its weight-carrying capability and its long-range endurance. His airplane was heavily loaded with ordnance including bombs and rockets and a tremendous amount of fuel. He was visiting Ie Shima to pass on his expertise to all of the young P-47 pilots, many of whom were out by the runway that morning to watch him take off. He planned to stay aloft for something like fourteen hours. They watched him open up the big 2,000 horsepower Pratt & Whitney engine to its full power, then they saw the puff of black smoke shoot out behind his airplane as he applied the water injection. About halfway down the runway, his engine missed, coughed and sputtered. At that split second, the pilot must make the fateful decision — go or no go. Chop the throttle, hit the brakes and hope for the best or pour on the coal and still hope for the best. He chose the latter. It turned out to be the wrong decision. Toward the end of the runway, his engine failed. He was traveling at least 100 miles an hour but didn't have flying speed. The big heavily-loaded P-47N went off the end of the runway and cliff (which were one and the same), cartwheeling to the rocks below. Everything went off like the Fourth of July. The young P-47 pilots who had come out to be inspired went back to their tents saddened but wiser. They had witnessed a powerful demonstration.

The specter of engine failure on takeoff haunted all of us. It wasn't that our mechanics weren't skilled and conscientious because they were. But they were waging a relentless battle against jungle humidity, coral dust and a constant shortage of replacement parts.

We figured if an engine was going to fail, it would most likely do so at maximum power so the sooner we got it to max power, the more runway we'd still have ahead of us. There's an old saying that the two most useless things to a pilot are the sky above and the runway behind. In line with that philosophy, we developed takeoff techniques similar to those used on carriers. We'd line up on the runway, press down on our toe brakes to lock our wheels, then ease the throttle all the way forward, pushing the manifold pressure up to sixty-one inches of mercury at 3000 RPM. If the engine was going to skip a beat, that would be the time. If it sounded and felt alright, you'd relax your toe pressure on the brakes and be on your way. This was all done very quickly for several reasons. You were only one airplane in a combat formation trying to get off the ground. There were airplanes ahead of you and behind you, and there were always other formations waiting to take off. And lastly, you had to be quick in that static runup because once that twelve-cylinder Rolls Royce Merlin reached full power you couldn't sit there and hold it.

The Pacific could be strikingly beautiful if we were in a mood to enjoy it. I always enjoyed the scenery more on the flights south, in the afternoons, rather than on those morning trips north to confront the enemy. Aside from any differences in our psychological outlook, the Pacific was more picturesque in the afternoons. On those many mornings, flying up to Japan, if the weather was clear, it was just that, but on those clear afternoons on our return trips, the Pacific and the East China Sea were truly magnificent. The vast oceans, reflecting the sparkling blue of the sky, would be punctuated by giant cumulonimbus clouds building up over each little island. Those towering clouds would have been a boon to early navigators if it were not for the fact that once formed, they would be carried out to sea by the moving air currents and would no longer identify the small chunks of land responsible for their creation. It was always a thrilling sight as our formations approached and flew past those towering cumulonimbus clouds. The larger and more strung-out our formations were, the more magnified became the perspective phenomenon. The white billowy columns rising from the surface to 40,000 feet literally dwarfed our P-51s, reducing the ones farthest away to mere specks.

In the mornings on the way north, even without the clouds to mark the islands, navigation was never a problem. We simply followed the chain of little islands which formed the Ryukus extending from Okinawa on the south to Japan on the north. As one island would disappear behind us, another one would soon come into view up ahead.

That morning as we approached Kyushu, we could see midway up its western coast, the ominous sign of a devastating bombing raid. A gigantic column of smoke, miles in diameter, rose straight up into the clear blue sky, transitioning from brown to white as it formed its own cumulonimbus cloud which must have reached 45,000 feet. It was truly an awesome sight. As we flew past, we could see the blackened remains of what had been an entire city. Our B-29s had been there during the night.

One thing we could always count on was being shot at whenever we got within range of their big guns. The black puffs were busting at our altitude but this time they were ahead of us. Usually they were behind us. Their big guns were directed by radar which would pick us up and then send its information to the guns which would aim accordingly and fire. We used a rule of thumb, to change course as often, in seconds, that we were high in thousands of feet. If we were flying at 15,000 feet, we'd change course every fifteen seconds. If we were at 10,000 feet, we'd change course every ten seconds. It seemed that it took that long for their radar and their guns to perform the complete cycle. But sometimes when the flak was particularly heavy, we'd modify that rule of thumb and do a lot of extra moving around. It might not have helped but it gave us something to do.

We arrived over Yawata and no mistaking, this had to be the place because the antiaircraft fire was intense. One by one, we rolled over and dived straight toward the blazing guns until we released our bombs and empty tank. With the airspeed right on the redline, those pullouts really unrolled our socks. We queued up offshore and headed for home. The young tigers had many phrases to describe flying at higher than normal power settings starting with, "pouring the coal to it," and, "hauling ass." Another much used expression was, "firewalling it" and, "balls out," which was modified into, "balls to the wall" and "testicles protruding."

High over the ocean on that trip south, I witnessed a contortionistic demonstration by my wingman which really gave me a laugh. On those long flights to and from Japan, we'd all just sit there in our cockpits and stare at each other, at our instruments, at the sky, at the ocean, and then back at each other. Well, this particular day, my wingman more than broke the monotony for me.

My first indication that something unusual was about to take place was the exessive squirming around that he was doing in his cockpit. A good-size man didn't have a surplus of room in a P-51 cockpit and he was a big man, but that didn't stop him.

I could see him moving around as he unfastened his seat

belt and shoulder straps. Next, he worked himself completely out of his parachute harness. Then off came his Mae West. P-51s weren't equipped with any sort of automatic pilot so his airplane inevitably did a few minor gyrations. On those long hauls, we always flew a loose relaxed formation so his extra bouncing around didn't endanger either of us, but it did magnify the moving around he was doing in his cockpit. I watched with utter fascination as he worked his way out of his flying suit. He unzipped it all the way to his crotch, then one at a time wrestled his arms out of it. He then raised up, arching his back to get it down around his legs. From my vantage point beside him and slightly forward, he appeared to be completely naked except for his helmet, goggles and oxygen mask. He was bent over doing some more wiggling, then he raised up and cranked his canopy open about four inches and commenced shoving something through the opening. The wadded-up olive drab object which he committed to the 300-mile-an-hour slipstream was his underwear shorts which obviously needed to be disposed. In addition to giving our skin a yellowish tint, our daily doses of Atabrine, supposedly to suppress malaria, acted on many of the troops as a strong laxative. That possibly could have been my wingman's trouble on that bright sunny afternoon high over the East China sea.

Sitting there looking at that totally naked pilot, except for his helmet, goggles and oxygen mask, I couldn't help but laugh. It was a good thing we had a long ways to go because he needed a lot of time to get everything back on again, except, of course, his long-gone shorts.

Every evening our tent was a particularly popular spot because we had the squadron's only radio, such as it was. Originally purchased quite some time before in Australia with money collected from all of the officers, it traveled with and was maintained by our squadron's communications officer, "Flywheel Miller", who happened to live in our tent. I never learned the origin of his nickname, but he sure was a whiz with electronics. The big black metal cabinet with all of its knobs and dials looked very impressive but when you lifted up the hinged top and looked inside, you'd see that two-thirds of the tube sockets were empty. Whenever a tube went bad, Miller would rewire it so that it would still function. On rare occasions we'd pick up the BBC being relayed from somewhere but the highlight of the evening was listening to Tokyo Rose.

One night, while several of the officers were sitting there, hearing the latest from Tokyo Rose, the flight surgeon happened to notice me huddled up on my cot shivering under a couple of blankets. Because it was warm shirtsleeve weather, he walked over, looked at me through the mosquito net and asked how I felt. I replied, "Not so good." He told me to come over to his tent the next morning if I didn't feel better.

With fever and chills and aching all over, I managed to drag myself over to see him the next morning. Finding that my temperature was 105, he said, "Get in my jeep and I'll drive you to the hospital." The "hospital" turned out to be a couple of larger tents over on the east end of our little island.

They stuck me in their contagious ward which didn't make me particularly happy. That seemed to be their standard procedure for high fevers that weren't yet diagnosed. So I spent the rest of that day and one night jammed in a tent with a lot of other sick men. I figured if I didn't already have something bad, I'd darn sure contract it in there.

That night we had our usual visitors. We could hear the bombs exploding and our own antiaircraft guns pounding back at them, but because we were on the opposite end of the island from their main objective, our parked airplanes, we couldn't really tell what was going on. I didn't feel like going out and watching so I just lay there and felt miserable.

Latrine rumors are as old and legendary as armies of the world, so it was fitting that the next morning, in the hospital's latrine, I would hear a new word — a word that I had never before heard. They were all talking about an "Atomic" bomb being dropped on Japan. I couldn't imagine what they were talking about. That word kind of sounded to me like it belonged with Buck Rogers.

My temperature had dropped back to normal so they let me go with the diagnosis of F.U.O., fever, undetermined origin. (The next time it was diagnosed as a severe case of malaria.)

When I arrived back at the squadron that morning, I learned the details of the night's bombing raid. For once their bombers got lucky and laid a string of bombs right along the revetments where our P-51s were parked, and completely destroyed ten of them.

While flying over the northeast part of Kyushu a couple of days later, we saw a gigantic blinding flash to the west of us. It was truly an eerie sight, like nothing any of us had ever seen before. On countless occasions we had seen the shockwaves radiating from the conventional bombs dropped by our heavy bombers, but the shockwave we saw on that April ninth morning was unlike anything we had ever seen before. It actually traveled through our formation. I know it was an optical illusion, but the skin on the next airplane seemed to ripple as the shockwave went past. We knew that we had just witnessed the detonation of a second atomic bomb.

There was no possible way that a country could endure for long the relentless pounding that our mighty air force was inflicting upon Japan. First it was military installations, then factories and finally entire cities that were being literally blown off the face of the earth.

The stage was being set for the mammoth invasion of Japan. Our tiny island was being crammed to capacity with combat aircraft and support personnel. Similar situations were developing at the airstrips on Okinawa next door, and on Iwo Jima about 900 miles to our east.

Rumors of Japan's intent to surrender persisted and finally on the night of August 14th, Tokyo Radio announced that Japan was ready to surrender. Our combat activities were suspended for a couple of days. Then one night a mission schedule was posted, just as had been on hundreds of preceding nights. My name was one of the eight listed to fly that next day. Needless to say, we were a little curious.

The purpose of our mission was explained during the

preflight intelligence briefing. Word had filtered down through channels that Japan had agreed to an unconditional surrender, but the U.S. wanted to verify whether or not they were really through. That was where we came in. We would be carrying a 500-pound bomb under one wing and an external fuel tank under the other. We were to fly up to Kyushu, then drop down to about one hundred feet above the ground, and slow down to about 200 miles an hour and fly directly over all of their eastern coastal defense antiaircraft gun installations to see if they would shoot at us. If any of them fired on us, we were instructed to bomb and strafe them.

There was quite understandably a certain amount of anxiety on our part and I'm sure those Japanese soldiers were equally concerned. As we slowly flew directly over their gun installations, we could actually see their faces. They were at their stations, but their guns never moved to track us. We completed the circuit with no shots being fired so our anxiety gave way to happiness realizing that World War II must really be over. We banked our P-51s south toward Ie Shima, and when well out to sea, jettisoned our bombs. That had to be the very last combat mission flown in World War II.

On August 19th, 1945, the stage was set for the surrender envoys to come from Japan. They were instructed to use two of their twin-engine Betty bombers which were to have all of their guns removed. They were to be painted white and to have green crosses painted on the sides of their fuselages, on their vertical tails and on their wings, top and bottom. They were to be escorted from Japan to Ie Shima by P-38s and P-61s. Those two types of aircraft were picked to prevent any recognition errors because the Japanese had no twin-boom fighter type aircraft. We all turned out to witness their arrival.

Right on schedule the bizarre formation appeared. The

escorting P-38s and P-61s peeled off and the two white Betty bombers circled the field, lowered their wheels and landed. As we stood beside the runway that warm August day, many of us wearing shorts and T-shirts, one thing struck us as kind of strange. The Japanese aircrews were all wearing leather fur-lined flying suits and helmets, just like in the movies. We did have to concede one point though and that was their airplanes must have been pretty drafty because there were gaping holes where the guns had been removed. The sixteen officers and men in the surrender entourage were decked out in their finest winter uniforms, replete with shiny boots and scabbarded samurais. They were ushered over to the waiting Douglas C-54 transport for the last leg of their journey, to Manila to meet with General MacArthur's Chief of Staff, to formalize the wording of the actual surrender documents.

The war was finally over. Most of our ground personnel, who had been overseas for at least a couple of years, would be going home. What was left, the pilots, the airplanes and a skeleton ground crew, would soon be moving up to Japan. That presented Henry and Wyper with one minor problem. We had a sailboat to dispose of.

We were sailing along parallel to the beach one afternoon discussing that very problem when some sailors on a beached LCT hollered at us about our boat. We looked at each other as if to say, we had found the answer. We came about, sailed up alongside the LCT and grabbed the line they threw to us. Although the front end of their ship was on the beach with its ramp/door down, the aft end was still well out in deep water. They laid a Jacob's ladder over the side to which we tied our boat, then we climbed aboard. LCT stands for Landing Craft Tank. It was a craft just large enough to carry one tank and to put it ashore. Its skipper was a young ensign. The rest of the crew, probably nine or ten, were all enlisted men. They were definitely interested. The ensign told us that he would like to have it for his crew's recreation. We said, "Fine, what do you have that you could trade for it?" We suggested maybe a case of beer. The ensign said they had no beer on board but they would give us a case of coke. We said O.K. and told him that we would come back later with a jeep to pick it up. Before we left, the ensign very briefly disappeared, then reappeared in a pair of shorts and was starting to go down the ladder to his newly acquired boat. We told him that as small as it looked, it really needed two men to handle it because of the round hull and lack of a good keel. He said, "I used to sail a star on the lakes back home. I'll be able to handle it." He went on down the ladder, got into the boat and cast off. Henry and I walked through the LCT's open front end and on up the beach.

We showered, got dressed, borrowed a jeep and drove back to the beach to pick up our case of coke. As we drove into the empty LCT, we noticed the entire crew was lined up along the aft rail staring out to sea.

In the fading light, I could barely make out something on the horizon. One of the sailors loaned us the ship's binoculars. I couldn't believe my eyes. The sails were down and the ensign was in the water trying to pull the boat. His futile efforts were of course to no avail. Somebody in the beach master's little watchtower was apparently also witnessing the drama because it wasn't much longer before an LCVP (Landing Craft, Vehicles and Personnel) was dispatched to the rescue.

The landing craft arrived on the scene and its driver/coxswain pulled the ensign from the water. They tied a line on the little boat and then started out in their usual manner — wide open. The surge and wake from the much larger landing craft was going to pull the little sailboat right under. After a couple of attempted starts, they cast it off and headed back to the beach without it. Our little sailboat had been set adrift in the East China Sea. We picked up the case of coke, put it in our jeep and departed.

I've often wondered about the ultimate fate of our little sailboat. We had done our best to make it unsinkable. It might have drifted to some distant shore to puzzle its finders, especially if they were natives of a less sophisticated land and didn't know the strange ways of very young fighter pilots.

The majority of our enlisted personnel had left for the states so maintenance on our airplanes was almost nonexistent. We probably had one mechanic for every ten airplanes. What was left of our organization packed up for the move to Japan. As on our previous moves, the ground personnel, vehicles and support equipment departed about a week earlier by ship. All that remained were the pilots, the P-51s and the few tents left standing into which we all moved.

The morning of our scheduled departure, we piled our personal belongings in a truck for delivery to the C-47 which would haul it to Japan. So all we had left were the poplin flying suits we were wearing, our shoes and socks, helmets, goggles, oxygen masks, Mae Wests and parachutes. Thinking that it might be kind of cool that night in Japan, I also kept my flight jacket.

During the war we had made numerous flights up to Japan and back by ourselves, but on this last trip we were going to be escorted by a "Pathfinder", a North American B-25 bomber, which was carrying some of the top brass from group headquarters. As ridiculous as that was, the B-25 was going to "show us the way".

Before climbing into my airplane, I laid my flight jacket in the bucket seat because I wouldn't be needing it on the flight. We fired up our engines and taxied out toward the runway.

We pulled up short of the runway for our customary pre-takeoff checks. I ran my engine up to 2300 RPM, with the propeller control full forward, then I switched from both magnetos to left and wow! The engine sputtered, coughed and nearly quit. I quickly switched back to both. Then I tried the right mag by itself. It was O.K. The RPM drop was acceptable. I switched back to both and ran the engine a little higher hoping to clear the plugs on the left mag if they were fouled. The Merlin engines were notorious for fouling spark plugs. Then I tried it again. It was no better. My left mag was sick. Under normal circumstances there would have been no second thoughts. You'd simply call the leader and tell him your engine was running rough and return it to its parking place so the crew chief could start working on it. But today was different. If I aborted that flight, my airplane would have to be transferred to one of the other groups still on Ie Shima. All of our personnel and all of our equipment were gone. We were the very last to leave. If I stayed, I wouldn't even have a place to sleep that night.

We took off, joined up into one huge formation and headed north to rendezvous with the B-25 which had taken off earlier.

As we approached the B-25, we started slowing down but not quickly enough because we went sailing right past, so after making a wide 360-degree turn, the formation drew up alongside. We had everything pulled back and my one-mag engine didn't like flying that slow. Apparently the one set of working plugs was starting to foul because it was getting rougher by the minute. I called the leader to get permission to pull out of the formation so I could use higher power settings. This was a peculiarly unique situation for us because our leader wasn't the man in the number one P-51. He was the colonel riding in the B-25. An anonymous voice from the B-25 told me that I could leave the formation, but to make S turns above them rather than flying on ahead by myself. The higher power settings did help but it was still pretty rough. I was thinking to myself how ironic this was — that on my very last flight from Ie Shima to Japan, I would have my most serious engine problems.

I was paying particularly close attention to my manifold pressure gauge, watching for any significant drop, when a huge centipede crawled out onto the face of the instrument panel. Having an extremely rough engine wasn't bad enough, now I had a vicious-looking centipede to contend with. It was as big around as my little finger and about six inches long. It was walking right across the face of my instruments. I wanted to smash it but I didn't want to bust my instruments, so with my gloved fist, I pressed against it thinking that it would fall onto my right rudder track where I could then step on it. Well, it didn't work out that way. As I withdrew my gloved fist it fell but not straight down onto the rudder track. Instead, it fell rearward, dropping down between my right side and the side of the fuselage, into a space of only a few inches. But my darn flight jacket was down there laid across my bucket seat, underneath my folded-up life raft, which was fastened to my parachute harness. That flight jacket was sticking out on both sides of my seat, almost to the side of the cockpit, which would very likely trap the centipede, preventing it from falling through to the bottom of the fuselage. With that happy thought I resumed my vigil of the rough-running engine.

Our final destination was Itami Airfield on the outskirts of Osaka, on the main island of Honshu, but we planned a lunch stopover at an airfield at Kanoya, on Kyushu, which was already occupied by another P-51 outfit. After we landed and parked our airplanes, I hunted down one of their mechanics and had him come out to my airplane to see if he could locate my trouble. I helped him remove the cowl and there it was. A stream of oil was running down from the rear of one of the valve covers, right into the magneto. He took the cover off the magneto and wiped it out, but said that he couldn't solve the problem because he didn't have any valve-cover gaskets to replace the one which was leaking. At least it would be a while before the magneto would fill up with oil again.

After we got the cowl back on and all buttoned up, I spent a few minutes looking for my little poisonous traveling companion. I shook out my flight jacket but it wasn't there so that meant it had to be somewhere else in my cockpit.

While I was helping the mechanic with my airplane, the P-51s of the 342nd Fighter Squadron took off on the last leg of their journey.

By this time it was getting late in the day and I wanted to get going but I didn't have a map. I thought maybe I could pick one up at the little flight operations shack when I filed my flight plan. I went in and asked if I could get a map of the area. They didn't have any but there was one on the wall so I went over and looked at it for a while. Not having a map, I planned a foolproof route. I'd fly northeast from Kanoya until I hit the coast of Kyushu, then I'd fly up the coast until I could see the island of Shikoku. I'd cross the Bungo Strait, pick up the west coast of Shikoku, fly north until I could see the southern coast of Honshu, then cross the Inland Sea, turn right and start looking for Kobe and Osaka. The sun was setting so I had to hurry. I asked for a form to make out my flight plan. While I was filling it out, two pilots came in and asked for a flight plan form. The operations officer asked what they were flying.

They said a C-47. The ops officer said, "Sorry, no C-47 departures after 5 p.m." The two pilots saw me filling out my flight plan and asked me what I flying. I told them a P-51. They seemed justly surprised that they couldn't take off with their twin-engine transport, but a single-engine fighter could. It surprised me too, but I wasn't about to question the system and I darn sure wasn't going to wait around in the event they might reconsider. Those C-47 pilots would really have been surprised had they known that I didn't even have a map.

I took off and headed northeast. There was enough twilight to see my checkpoints. I eventually picked up the southern coast of Honshu just west of what I figured must be Kobe. I identified the sprawling city of Osaka, looked north and a little to the west and there were the concrete runways of what must be Itami Airfield. By now it was almost totally dark. I was at 3,000 feet, indicating about 380 miles per hour so I shoved the nose down, aiming right at the intersection of runways. Indicating nearly 500 miles an hour, I pulled up into a huge Immelmann. As I rolled out at the top, I pressed my mike button and asked, "Itami Airfield, do you see a P-51?" A very bored voice replied, "Yes, you just did an Immelmann over the field, cleared to land, runway two-five." I came back around, pitched out, lowered my wheels and flaps and landed. It was now pitch-black. The tower directed me to the area where the other P-51s were parked. Using my landing light, I found them and a place to park. After shutting down the engine, I turned on the map light and filled out the aircraft's form-one, noting that the left valve-cover gasket was leaking oil into the magneto and that there was a centipede in the cockpit, somewhere. I turned off the light and the master switch and climbed out of the airplane. I was clear across the field from the tower and there wasn't a soul in sight anywhere.

I climbed back into my P-51, turned on the master and the radio and called the tower, asking them to send a vehicle over to pick me up. I again turned everything off and closed the canopy. After a short wait, two headlights appeared coming down the runway.

The G.I. ambulance pulled up and I got in. The driver was not alone. He had a little pet spider monkey which reminded me of the late Tojo. I had not ridden in an ambulance since my midair back in New Mexico.

We arrived back at the airport's main building. I thanked him and asked if he knew where the 348th Fighter Group was quartered. He didn't. There were only a couple of other people in the building and they didn't know either. By this time I was getting kind of hungry. It had been a long time since breakfast back on Ie Shima. While my buddies were eating lunch at Kenoya, I was helping the mechanic to diagnose my engine problems.

One of the G.I.s told me their outfit was close by and that I could eat dinner in their messhall. Figuring that it would be more pleasant looking for my outfit on a full stomach, I graciously accepted his invitation.

After dinner, one of the fellows offered to take me in his jeep to look for my outfit. Asking about the 348th Fighter Group or the "P-51 outfit that arrived today" brought completely negative responses. Nobody had heard of them. We went from place to place asking everybody we saw. Then, as I was asking one group of officers, I happened to say "Colonel Banks' outfit." That brought an immediate response. They said,"Oh, Colonel Banks' outfit! Sure, we know where his outfit is." It seems that during the previous week, while he was making arrangements for our arrival, the group commander had become pretty well known.

Following the directions that were given to us, we drove through the narrow winding streets of Itami and finally came to a large rambling two-story structure which had a makeshift sign out in front identifying it as the home of the 348th Fighter Group.

I would see a little of Japan and then I would be going home.